1983

REVIEW COPY

Email: serlynportal@yahoo.ca

1983
The Unknown Season

TOBIAS MAXWELL

1983: The Unknown Season

Copyright © 2011 Tobias Maxwell. All rights reserved. No part of this book may be reproduced or retransmitted in any form or by any means without the written permission of the publisher.

Published by Libero Printemps Books
Cover photo by Jamie Pelino

ISBN: 978-0-9868764-0-0

Direct any author inquiries to:
Serlyn Portal Management
277 Manning Ave.
Toronto, ON M6J 2K8
Phone: (416) 364-9916 Fax: (416) 364-8536
Email: serlynportal@yahoo.ca

for Lillian

life lived is life loved,
time here is much too brief
for the unknown season.

Foreword

Most people's lives are quite interesting, some more so than others. Over the years friends who have read excerpts from my diaries and journals have often encouraged me to publish them. This book is the culmination of that encouragement.

I chose this year to start with because 1983 represents a demarcation of sorts in my nearly forty years of daily diaries. The years of debauchery that thrived during my time in Montreal, Toronto and New York City all came to a head in Santa Fe. And though it would continue unabated, on and off for some years to come, change *was* looming.

Memory being what it is, this book could not exist had I not bothered to write it all down on paper. Writing it down in real time is what, hopefully, makes this account worth reading. I make no apologies for my actions. The man I was then is certainly not the man I am today, but a part of me, as memory goes. This diary and its accompanying journal are an accurate record of that long ago journey, my unknown season.

The Week of
December 27th
to
January 2nd

Monday: (see 1982)

Tuesday: (see 1982)

Wednesday: (see 1982)

Thursday: (see 1982)

Friday: (see 1982)

Saturday: Welcome 1983. Sounds ominous. To think that come next September, a decade will already have gone by since I met Monsieur, the same weekend I'd moved from Montreal to Toronto. Last night's New Year's festivities went very well. The disco was quite large, air conditioned and well lit. All the rooms we've gone to here in Acapulco have been reminiscent of 1940s nightclubs, at least how those clubs are portrayed in the movies. The day was spent in pursuit of our last sun and swim. Bought stuffed armadillo. Coo hates it. I christened him "Rrrocky" from all the ads on the local radio promoting the Stallone film. The blond Frenchman seems a thing of the past. Probably all for the better! Can't wait to get back to Santa Fe and start to work on *From Now On*.

Sunday: Everything does come to pass. We finally left Acapulco with its beautiful views and were back into the chaos of traveling. Lines, lines and more lines and delays. Listening to men talking while we were in line at the airport made me realize how atypical my marriage is with Coo. Not that this is any surprise! Had leg spasms on the plane all the way from Houston to Albuquerque. It was deadly cold when we got back to Santa Fe. Had no employment info but did have 3 messages from Monsieur on the answering machine.

The Week of
January 3rd–9th

Monday: First full day back trying to get things in order. Did banking, shopping and picked up our cats. Went to look at the house on Calle don Jose. I want it *so* badly. Se. called at night, spoke for quite a long time. Barry Yellen confirmed that the closing of our building had finally occurred. Now for the monies to come through from the sale of our co-op! I wrote the first ten pages of *From Now On* and started to clean up *Cooperative Murder*.

Journal – Jan. 3rd, 1983

This date, or at the very least this year, seems ominous, a witness to time's bittersweet scheme—this forever moving forward without any capacity to delay any of it. This onwards motion, never to return. That's where these jottings come in, I guess; they leave behind minutia of the days' stay, enabling me the luxury to travel back in time.

Without the insight that these journeys hopefully bring—where would I be . . .

We've just returned from Acapulco. The rampant poverty seemed more acute down there. It felt foreign, though if we traveled our own country far and wide, I'm sure we'd find bleak patches of squalor here as well. How can anyone fight the good fight against socialism when faced with such inequality?

Coo and I want so very much to buy that house at 134 Calle Don Jose. It has the space and the charm that we seek. Of course we'd need to find some kind of gainful employment to qualify for a mortgage loan out here.

These days, I face the challenge of putting the finishing touches to Cooperative Murder *and then I need to plunge into this new project* From Now On. *Not till that book, that vision of Tim's life is written down will I rest easy. To do that would feel like a big accomplishment. Now whether it'll be good is another matter all together.*

Tuesday: And so our routine is back. Up, out and about on errands. I sent out letter for word processor job, and Coo applied for a hostess gig. Also spoke to a guy at the co-op newspaper about ad sales job. Oy vey. Nothing at the penitentiary till Thursday. At night, my local visit to the adult bookstore (ABS) proved fruitful, though the town's smallness frightens me. Everyone here wants to go home with each other. What happened to plain, honest to goodness anonymous sex!

Wednesday: Back to the food co-op for our weekly stint. Work always goes so quickly. Spoke to Lo. Li. who sounded pleasant, if a little bit tense. Bought glass frames but can't tell if I can pull off the look. No monies in hand yet but we did put in our offer on the house. Swim at night was so-so, but ABS had a great picture, breathtakingly erotic. Sipping Kahlua and trying to write, such a cliché.

Journal – Jan. 5th, 1983

The dream of being published is a constant that rarely diminishes, especially these days, now that I've created the semblance of a writer's routine. I sit here in my room, often freezing cold, trying to warm up as I read, write, think, then jot some more things down.

Speaking with Lo. Li. today was interesting. It was night and day from when we spoke before. It's not that I don't want to work with this woman, it's just that the time and the situation don't feel right at this juncture. Putting in our offer today on the house wasn't all that frightening. It'll only become more so when/if they accept our offer. Today, just now, I feel as though I could conquer the world. Amazing what an ounce of liqueur will to do one's sense of self! Ah, ego.

As for my mad attraction to pornography, I simply give in to it, like friendly dirt that children love to play in. Different dirt, and not a child any longer . . . Or am I?

Thursday: Went out for early interview for co-op ad rep. It went all right but I wonder if any real money can be made at this. Did most of the calling that needed done. Nothing in Reserve Fund from B. Yellen. Tackled tax material for capital gains issue. They make it so damn complicated to get at the end numbers. At night we went over to meet Na. & El. Ma., two of the most original and likeable people I've met in a while. Their age alone makes them quite precious, but their ideas, the accrued reading between the two, makes them that much more fascinating.

Friday: The days are gone before I know it. Ju. T. cancelled her afternoon Hebrew lesson. Nothing from the money market and nothing from Savings and Loan. No news is good news, I guess. Writing and editing. Went for eye examination and ordered yet another pair of glasses. Mail is too sporadic. People don't like to write anymore it seems.

Saturday: Saw *The Verdict*. Good film but audience sucked, with loud obnoxious kids that shouldn't have even been there. A woman snored behind me on and off throughout the movie. Got stoned at night and enjoyed being out of it after abstaining for the last few weeks.

Sunday: Went and auditioned for production of *Romeo and Juliet*. Prospects are good that I might get the lead. Little or no monies involved, and likely no Equity contract. Worth taking a chance? Finished latest revision of *Coopera-*

tive Murder. Now to type it up. Finished the rest of part I of *From Now On*. It feels too slow, I can just sense it.

The Week of January 10th–16th

Monday: (*NB. This year's diary was a Virginia Woolf themed book. The week's quote was *"The mind is like a dog going round and round to make itself a bed. So, give me new and detestable ideas, I will somehow trample a bed out of them."*) New ideas, yes those would help, especially as it concerns my poetry. Can't seem to write anything of substance in poetry form these days. Was it all just a youthful phase for some fifteen years or so?! Went for callback for *R. and J.* and was offered the role of Romeo. Okay, now for that challenge. The cast may be a bit better than I thought or expected. Nice people . . . new friends? Spoke to B. Yellen. Our money is on the way. No unemployment insurance yet.

Tuesday: Finished reading *Inside Looking Out* by H. Lemay. His upbringing seems and sounds more French Canadian than mine was. Where does my true identity lie? Life, as I know it, is but confusion, with happiness a constant relative that eludes me even as I hear it knock. That blond diver was at the pool again tonight, making his presence felt in fairly obvious ways.

Wednesday: Days speeding by quite quickly. Did our core work at co-op, came home and changed, then went to Savings and Loan for our meeting only to be informed that someone else with "earnest" money had bid higher than us.

We left and then returned and got into a heated argument about business practices. The man in charge refused to budge. At night, I went to our first play reading. Not bad. People seemed pleased. Met a lot of folks. Spoke with Carr. and Nor. to see about trying to get an Equity guest artist contract for me.

Thursday: Up early to sell advertising. It's okay but I'm not exactly wowing them! Monies were deposited into money market fund today. Finally, the end of a four-year ordeal. Set up an appointment time with the penitentiary guys. Gave my first Hebrew lesson to Ju. T. today. It went very well. Mrs. F. would be proud. Started doing work on our taxes.

Friday: Slept in. Went to meet with a client for ad sales. Paid phone bill, rented **IBM** Selectric. Typed up first chapter. Looks and feels good. Spoke with Mk. Pa. briefly and set up time with Pl. for fencing tomorrow. At pool, that young blond guy was there. God, he is beautiful. At ABS, I met this guy from before. I'm always amazed at how strangers can share such intimacy.

Saturday: A full day filled with appointments. At night, I went to take a fencing lesson with these two guys from the college up on the mountain. St. John's? Very nice place. I'd have attacked one of the guys, had he been so inclined to indulge. Pl. came too, and as nice as he is, he worries much too much for my tastes. As for Mk. Pa., I feel myself attracted by the friendship but I need to keep an eye out so as not to let any flame begin to kindle there. It would be futile. Got stoned.

Sunday: Slept in. Did some typing and exercised. Stayed in to learn lines. Spoke to Carr. Equity letter came in and we're lunching on Wednesday to see how to make it work with as little hassle as possible.

The Week of
January 17ᵗʰ – 23ʳᵈ

Monday: Each day the mail brings little or nothing at all. U.I. benefits will never come through, I fear. The rain trickled abysmally all day long. Coo and I splurged and bought a couch, along with a chaise longue with matching ottoman. It should look nice with the adobe style of the house. Once again, I bought myself yet another desk. This time, I feel it'll be mine for a long time. Co. Mi.'s letter hasn't arrived but I spoke with her and she did say she'd mailed it. Wrote to Monsieur.

Tuesday: I'm not diligent enough in filling these pages on time. The days are done and gone, and I don't set myself the time to even write out what I did, let alone permit myself the time to self-reflect. If not here, at least I'm writing more in my journal pages. I do luxuriate in staying home and typing away. Went for a swim. Saw *Dark Crystal* at night.

Journal – Jan. 18ᵗʰ, 1983

Your days are most definitely numbered, I'm afraid. Here I sit, writing at my new wooden desk with ample space to spread out. I could use tons more filing cabinets and bookcases but this is the lap of luxury compared to my past living spaces. What with my newly rented

IBM Selectric, I'm set. The novella is slowly being typed up; not as long as I'd imagined, I'm afraid. But there's such satisfaction that it shadows everything else. Between being cast as Romeo in the Romeo and Juliet *production, the book, Mk. Pa.'s new friendship and the monies from our sale of our co-op back in New York City, I should be able to sit back and relax. Hard as it may seem and harder to believe, it is not the easiest task to accomplish.*

Wednesday: Up at a ghastly hour to do our food co-op shift. Got home and typed before meeting Carr. for lunch. It went okay. In the afternoon, Coo and I shopped for a carpet and ordered a chair to match the new couch. You only live once! Got an hysterically funny letter from Co. Mi. At night, I rehearsed fencing with Mk. Pa. up at St. John's. We never stopped laughing. He taught me some Spanish slang. I taught him some Hebrew.

Thursday: Busy day. Gave Ju. T. her Hebrew lesson. Then I attended a co-op sales rep meeting. Met Chr. Learning my lines is coming along very slowly. No mail. Went swimming. That blond diver was there. How do I try to approach him? Pot plants finally sprouted. Mk. Pa. came over and we watched a movie. He likes Coo, I can tell.

Journal – Jan. 20th, 1983

Well I can say that I'm experiencing those vital statistics, those precious emotions attached to falling in love. The good news is—I think—I'm being mature and I'm going to hold back.

It's all so very strange. Lust doesn't enter into it yet. I'm just slowly finding myself being absorbed by the all-imposing, all-consuming powers of love. This falling in love/like can only be compared to catching a virus, something that needs to be worked out of the system.

And it will.

It's something that I think I'll be able to handle sanely enough. I fear, however, that I may have screwed up the friendship between Da. Ml. and me. Our parting tonight seemed rough with his slamming the car door like he did. It was loud, and it resonated inside the car. My imagination? I don't think so. Will wait and see . . . But I'm usually not wrong at spotting anger in others, no matter how subliminal or subdued it is.

Friday: I repeat myself way too much. And . . . *as if* I'm going to change at this stage of the game! Stayed in to type away and to learn my lines. Bought swimming goggles and went to the pool. It was almost empty. Got stoned and watched Second City. Co. Mi. called us in the morning. It was nice to hear her voice. I really do miss her company.

Saturday: Slept in, typed and then learned lines. Went to look at eyeglasses and then at some lovely homes, one, an old historic beauty, and the others, gorgeous condos. We went out at night to celebrate our 2nd official (3rd in actuality) wedding anniversary. Had a nice meal. Coo had her period so she wasn't in the mood to fuck. Anyway, it was too damn cold. Drank lots of wine instead.

Sunday: Typed and then went swimming with Mk. Pa. I just like him a lot. I'm not interested in him sexually, only erotically. Does that even make sense? At night went out for coffee with Ju. T. It's so nice to go out and not worry about funds. Oh lord, I know how fortunate we are. If only my writing could get us somewhere!

The Week of
January 24th – 30th

Monday: Another week to take on. Finally finished typing up *Cooperative Murder*. It's not as long as I'd hoped but happy with it for now. Sent monies off to both sets of parents. Went swimming. Afterwards, I dropped by ABS and met a real live cowboy. I was beside myself and acted accordingly. What can I say . . . next!

Tuesday: Okay, let's see what I did with my day . . . No monies in the mail. Sent off picture and resumes to Actor's Guide. Coo got a job at this lunch joint downtown. I hope she can survive that hectic pace. Lines are slowly coming along. Started calling places for March issue ads. Modeled at night for Ely Levin's group. Don't like the atmosphere much.

Wednesday: A very long day. Up for co-op duties in the cheese department and caught a coffee with Coo before going off to seek out more info on our pot plants. Found some good books at the state library. I need to read more on the subject. Bought some planting things and set up a greenhouse system with hopefully better success to come of it in the future. Carr. came over and we signed my Equity contracts. He wants to use my picture for publicity.

I cooked using the new wok for Na. & El. Ma. who came over for dinner. Love their company. If I had more money I'd take them to Europe.

> ### *Journal – Jan. 26th, 1983*
>
> *A happy day. Actors' Equity Association gave the okay for my guest artist contract for me to do the R. & J. production. I feel good about that.*
>
> *We had the Mainvilles over and that went quite well. Every step of the way is getting easier and better for me. I need to enjoy this rather magical time in my life. Growing our two pot plants, learning my lines, writing books, drinking a little now and then. Interesting how the pictures with Na. and El. Ma. had me smiling again. That's a nice switch!*
>
> *What's amiss, I'm afraid to admit, is Coo and me. We had our first major discussion about being ourselves more and having to live our own lives. I expressed my fear that she may not be living her life to its fullest potential with me around. It was a heavy conversation. It's hard, more so for her than for me. I wonder why that is? I'm no less feeling than her. I don't understand that one yet . . . Or do I?*
>
> *She's in the bedroom now, trying to hold back tears. Does this mean the beginning of the end for our marriage scenario? Where do we go from here?*

Thursday: Dropped off fact sheets for March issue of co-op magazine. Gave Ju. T. her Hebrew lesson. Drove Coo to model at Ely Levin's, then I went swimming. Dropped by the ABS, but of course! Bad habits never die.

Friday: Got a check from our NYC landlord for Coo's deposit. Unfortunately the car broke down and we had to have it repaired and there went the monies. Saw films at Museum of Folk Art. Excellent subject matter. The film on Peking Circus made me want to juggle again. Met Na. & El. Ma. at the museum and we went to their place and looked at her artwork. She's a gifted artist; such beautiful collection of ink sketches. She gave me an ice cream machine they weren't using.

Saturday: Went to see Ge., the blond diver, in a swim meet. We spoke briefly but it was a little uncomfortable. Did shopping. At night, saw *Once Upon a Mattress*, which was "okay." Great actress playing the Queen. The nurse in *R. and J.* was there and she introduced us to quite a few people. Came home and got stoned and video'd out. Made great love.

Sunday: Slept in. Mk. Pa. called early again. I felt bad, but what could I say?! We bumped into him on our way to see *Le Beau Marriage*. Okay film. Ju. T., Coo and I all went to the Soak for a bite to eat. Learning lines and trying to make some headway with *Cooperative Murder* edits.

The Week of
January 31ˢᵗ – February 6ᵗʰ

Monday: Read *Anais Nin* and *Perspectives on Porno*, neither as good as I'd hoped. It was a busy day of errands. Dropped by Mk. Pa.'s store and chatted for a while. Wrote a short story about George and Thelma, no title yet. Swam and went to ABS. Can't help myself. Coo and I talked of moving to LA next fall. Sounds good to me.

Tuesday: These lengthy lapses in my entries makes a diary's entries less accurate than they could be. No excuses. Zip in the mail. A snowstorm caused havoc with road conditions. Got car stuck in a ditch when I went to model for Larry and Albert. Had an okay class. Continuing to edit *Cooperative M*. Tedious task. It's hard to be objective.

Wednesday: Up early for our co-op stint. Coo goes off to work now and I have the luxury of my own space to indulge myself. We're slowly getting over some rough spots in this marriage. Cancelled my fencing workout with Mk. Pa. due to sore hand and back. A. Buresch called to express her doubts about playing Juliet in *R. & J*. Spoke to Bb. and we offered the role of Juliet to Stacy who said she'd consider it. Our car broke down again and we had to rent another car.

Thursday: The notes from V. Woolf's calendar inside this diary certainly inspire the writer in me to dream big. Finishing what edits I can do on *Cooperative Murder*, I dream way too much about this. It's such a miniscule accomplishment. Decided on "Desperate Errands" for yesterday's short story. Modeled, and taught Ju. T. her 4th Hebrew lesson. Ate some grass at night and started talking about the feasibility of doing a two-person show with Coo. Car repair wasn't as expensive as we'd originally been told.

Friday: Power failure overnight set us back a bit in the morning, with Coo being late for work because of it. I did some errands, then some shopping with Coo after her workday. The *Co-op Newspaper* came in with some of my ads. Went to Bach variations at night, a nice concert. Considering applying for a job at the co-op newspaper. Not sure if I have the qualifications.

Saturday: Up early for brunch preparations. Stacy didn't show up at first so we invited our neighbor across the way, Evelyn, to come over. Stacy finally showed up very late, flowers in hand, along with an apology. I had to leave them to go fencing. The practice went quite well. Mk. Pa. was in a mood though. Stacy was still home when I got back. She can't do *R. & J.* though, since she's planning a move to NYC. Bought a small couch for our guest room. Got stoned at night and discussed the possibilities of going to Paris later in the spring. Why not!

Sunday: Slept away the day. I got up in the late afternoon and did some edits on *Cooperative Murder*. Getting ready to possibly send out query letters. Started looking at where I might submit this.

The Week of
February 7th – 13th

Monday: A big week here. Got up early for unemployment meeting. It went very fast and it got me nowhere. Submitted "Desperate Errands" to one place. At night, *R. & J.* reading went very well, especially when considering that two of our main characters were missing. A. Buresch did show up towards the end.

Tuesday: Wrote an article that I want to submit to the *Co-op Newspaper*. Rehearsal was very slow but it began to pick up along the way.

Journal – Feb. 8th, 1983

The pages of this book, my fifth journal, are almost at the end. I finished reading the last of the biography on George Sand—an interesting life, so full of what I crave. Can I even begin to compose mine yet?

The times we live in today are much more complex. In many ways it's more difficult to make one's mark. Where are the revolutions one could sign on for? My love affairs of the past are all gone. My marriage, a liaison that though filled with some contentment, strikes me as a petty bourgeois state that seems too easy an out for me.

Trying to indulge my art, I fear of becoming too self-indulgent. Romeo and J. *rehearsals have me facing a challenge like none in my recent past. My first short novella written and begging to be sent out, as well as some short stories. My poetry lies dead in a file cabinet, and my acting career going where? What do the stars have in their sights for me?*

At least the rent is paid and the next few years should be less hectic than the previous ones. Will whatever sanity is ours let us enjoy it or will we be unable to cope with our new monetary fortune, changed so drastically with the sale of our co-op? On to other pages . . .

Wednesday: The days just blend into one long day. Wrote poem "Confining Journey". Called home to tell mom not to send us monies. Rehearsal went very well.

Thursday: Didn't have much to do today. Mk. Pa. came over in the morning. Had a nice chat. Did a bit of shopping later on. Such a luxurious day.

Friday: A day mostly to myself. Slept in. Did my exercises. Found a dog outside of the supermarket, with gum stuck all over his fur. Called SPCA to pick him up. We may be adopting him. Decided to call him Johnny for now. The Albuquerque agent called but the part was really not right for me. I went swimming after a long time away. Saw *Zoot Suit*. Great images. Got stoned at night.

Saturday: A week of new responsibilities come to an end. Everything was fine till today when emotions flared up and Coo and I exchanged heated words. The one positive outcome, at least, is that it decreases the building resentment between us. I'm at such a good time in my life and I don't even realize it. We have no real money worries and we still put ourselves constantly through the mill over finances. Force of habit, I guess.

Journal – Feb. 12th, 1983

Well, one more tiny entry in this fifth journal, I guess. Stoned just now. I had an intense exchange of words at rehearsal today. I hope things will be more settled from this point on. I do hope I didn't overstep my boundaries in speaking out like I did. At night, watching R. & J. on TV, it reassured me of the right direction I'm in.

Sunday: Slept in. Went to see Johnny at the shelter. We brought him a blanket and a chew bone. Called Se. back in Toronto. We spoke for over an hour. I wish I could just send him money for him to visit us. Went swimming. Spoke to both Pl. and to Bb., and things appear okay. Rehearsals have been pushed forward a day due to not having one last Friday for some reason, along with my upcoming absence.

The Week of
February 14th– 20th

Monday: Barely remember the days as I'm late, as usual, with this. Coo came home from work and had made Valentines of pressed flowers. Rehearsal went well. We redid some of the early scenes. I feel a cold coming on. Made up the invitations for our "slipper brunch." The color copies look great. We visited Johnny at the pound.

Tuesday: Felt really bad all day. Rehearsal was in shambles. All the extras were there and we didn't have a room big enough for the principals let alone this merry band of revelers. Tense to say the least. Johnny seems to have such a great disposition.

Wednesday: Didn't do co-op and I just slept away the day. Visited Johnny and went to rehearse.

Thursday: A long day of futility for me. The Denver, CO, audition went well for Coo but atrociously bad for me. And there were only two Equity theatres present in all. A precious amount of money wasted flying up for the day for that small of a hiring pool. We stayed in at night.

Managed to buy dog supplies on our way into town from Albuquerque.

Friday: My cold is set in. Picked up Johnny at the shelter and took him to get groomed. Did some errands. Rehearsal at night was okay but we wasted precious time with Pl. not knowing we'd moved over to the theatre space. We all sat around afterwards hanging out for a change.

Saturday: Up early with things to do. Drove Coo to her modeling booking. Mail brought news of Unemployment Insurance fuck-ups. The law firm back in NYC gave my W2 to Co. Mi. so I had to call her about it. She'd already mailed it to me. Had an okay rehearsal with Bb. and A. Buresch. The fencing practice, though, was a farce. The fight we'd already learned was cancelled and Doug taught me a new one. It's a little more dangerous and doesn't make much sense for now. Vibes weren't very pleasant, I thought.

Sunday: Slept in a little but Johnny went out early in the backyard. Such a good-natured animal. Took him for a nice long walk with Coo. Went to see *Missing*. Very well made. I think this was the movie that I auditioned for Costa Gravas back in early fall of 1977 when he was in Toronto. Not sure. Depressing content.

The Week of
February 21st – 27th

Monday: A bummer day. Brought Johnny in for his shots and he slipped on the vet's table. When we got him home he started acting up, crying and barking like a *wild* animal so I brought him back in. It seems he hurt some already damaged tissue in his leg, based on the X-ray. With little options that made any sense to us at all, given his age and the condition he apparently had, we gave the okay to put him to sleep. The guilt at perhaps being too quick in our decision will not leave me for a long while. Rehearsal wasn't bad. A group of us went out for coffee afterwards. A. Buresch speaks such beautiful French. Saw *Gandhi*, an incredible feat of movie making.

Tuesday: How productive are these days? Modeled for Al Handel et al. Stopped by ABS on my way home. Did some writing. Bought bookshelves and put them together. Coo had the car and drove me to rehearsals, which went very well. Doug is now doing a part!

Wednesday: Did Co-op in the AM and then came home to write but fell asleep before noon. It was a lazy day from there. Rehearsal was okay but seemed interminable with the entire mob present. Stayed up talking with Mns. till 2 AM. Interesting soul. Da. Ml. is quickly becoming closer.

Thursday: Got up to model for Al Handel. Only did portraiture this time and he finally paid me a decent wage. Went to deli and then home for Hebrew lesson with Ju. T. Proceeded to put up posters for *R. & J.* around town. Bumped into Bb. and later, Na. & El. Ma. Went into this neat shop looking for Coo's birthday present. Got to bed fairly early. Made love. Coo got her okay from Nl. to stay with him when she goes to Los Angeles.

Friday: Up very early to drive to Albuquerque. Our pieces went quite well. Picked up dance supplies for the show.

Got home to find that my rehearsal was cancelled—Bb. was sick, so I set up a rehearsal for Da. Ml. and A. Buresch. My heart is beating more quickly when I'm in this man's presence! Good rehearsal. Came home and crashed late.

Saturday: Had an early morning rehearsal in the theatre. What a luxury. Da. Ml.'s reaction to my present of his own hat was confusing. How off am I in my infatuation with him? Dance and fencing rehearsals were a catastrophe. Mk. Pa. hit me so hard during one of the fight sequences I was sure my finger was busted. Ate some grass at night and went out for a bite and a soak. Got to bed very late.

Sunday: Woke up 10 minutes before we were supposed to be at Ju. T.'s. We got her off to NYC on her way to live in Israel. Goodbye to a crazy, lovely lady. Came home and tried to nap. Then over to Na. & El. Ma.'s for *tourtière*. God it was good. Stayed there till very late. Had a lovely time. Played instruments. Came home only to find out that my costume fitting is cancelled for tomorrow.

The Week of
February 28th – March 6th

Monday: Unemployment insurance is a farce. Bought Cuisinart food processor and went wild making a Chinese wok supper. Rehearsals progress slowly but surely. Da. Ml. was there. He said something very sweet about loving—I expect he was referring to the Friar for Romeo. But then who knows . . .

Journal – Feb. 28th, 1983

"Who am I?" What a great and confident beginning to a new journal, my sixth to be exact. The book looks so business-like on the outside, so efficient. I wish that I could say the same about my state of mind. Of course it's the usual id business that's plaguing me.

On this last day of this short second month of the year, I find myself at odds with my tastes, my pursuits.

I'm a married man and I do love my wife. Yet here I am playing Romeo in a production of Romeo & J. *and I'm head over heels in love with the man playing Friar Lawrence. The reasons behind this infatuation should be weighed out very carefully before starting something I might regret later on.*

I guess I'm bored with the same old day in/day out routine of my life. And though I'm physically attracted to Da. Ml., it's not in my usual way. There's a bit more reality regarding a possible liaison with him. Yes, I have my doubts about whether I could sustain an affair with this man, let alone a relationship that might come of it. This is such a gargantuan decision.

There's none of the youthful "fuck it, I'm going for it" feeling here. Here's a man in his mid-thirties, with some of Se.'s qualities—which in itself should be a measure of caution—but he's a good writer with interesting perceptions on life, very intelligent and good looking. He's certainly someone I don't want to hurt, but is he someone I want to love?

Hell, it's too late, I'm already in love with him!

There's nothing I can do about that. I'm like a schoolboy with a crush. My mind hasn't been so preoccupied by someone, not like this, for quite some time. But I don't even know if he's gay. I don't know if he feels like I do, if he happens to be gay. Or is it just a physical thing coming from his end?

Then that begs the question: Am I willing to settle for just that? Would I be okay with that? Of course no one knows what something is, what exists, until they've taken the plunge, opened up the door to see if it's happiness or misery beyond it.

This revolving door of possibilities sends me reeling for more solid answers. I've always liked the challenge of involvement, especially when life's seas are so calm. The need to pursue someone has always been in my makeup, but I think that this love for Da. Ml. is not simply for the pursuit of it. I think that at my age I can say that I'm able to recognize lust as the primary mover, while this feels more like love, one that's been nurturing for a while.

Will it grow to something bigger than life, or die the natural death of a seedling left to dry and wither from lack of attention . . . ?

Tuesday: Let's see, did I do anything specific today? Ah yes, went to the Santa Fe Opera to pick out props with Bb. and Da. Ml. came along. We were alone together for a few minutes on the freight elevator but nothing much transpired. The play is slowly getting there. Co. Mi. called from New York first thing in the morning.

Wednesday: Desperate to have Da. Ml. call me. Of course, he'll never call *that* way. Went to get our costumes, first at the Opera's warehouse, then over to their theatre. I'm happy with my costumes. I just worry that mine won't match up with the rest of the costumes. At night, rehearsal went okay but I couldn't seem to get into a position where I could approach Da. Ml. without making it look too obvious. I had an unfortunate incident with Mns.—I do believe he was *totally* stoned. I may be wrong but what else could explain such behavior?

Thursday: If I'm not careful, the weeks end up empty, without faces and identities of their own. Rehearsed the fight with Tybalt. Later in the evening, I finally confessed to Da. Ml. my feelings for him. It was incredible, the power of the passion I felt between us. We had coffee and dropped by his office afterwards. Gave Coo her birthday gift. Where are we going with this?!

Journal – March 3rd, 1983

Well dear Journal, how can I put it? How can I find the words to express the magnitude of my exuberance!

Like a young adolescent entering the folds of first true love I find all the magic and joy attached to the passions such a liaison brings. I finally made a gesture towards Da. Ml. and he reciprocated in kind.

After rehearsal we went for coffee to talk and then went over to his office. I'm totally enamored and smitten. I can't even seem to touch the ground, my heart is so full with the food of love. His eyes and face, his body, all is so beautiful. Of course we want to try and deal with this situation in a sensible manner. I have no desire to hurt Coo. God, how I don't want that! But I can't be dishonest to the point of lying and denying this to myself. I have no idea where all this will end, but I know that I can't stop now. I'm about to burst.

Friday: Coo's 30th birthday and what do I do? I write a love poem to Da. Ml., and hand-delivered it. He called me seconds before I had to leave for rehearsal. Well . . . here we go!! After rehearsal, Coo and I went to the Soak for a sauna and a very heavy conversation. I laid it out quite plainly, trying to make sure she knew exactly where I was at, of late. The harsh reality is that I'm falling madly in love with Da. Ml.

Journal – March 4th, 1983

I really don't have anyone that I can discuss this Da. Ml. situation with, no one close at hand.

Today is Coo's birthday and she's talking to all of her family and relatives. The responsibilities attached to heterosexual coupling can be hazardous to your health! The guilt at imagining my in-laws' reaction to a busted marriage is too powerful to ponder. My own parents' reaction might also be one I'm not prepared to handle— my father's, for sure. And yet, I find myself immersed in feelings that I cannot, do not want to control.

I am well aware of the price that might be paid for those feelings but they are not whimsical in nature, any more than the cacophony of birds that echoes outside, or the dogs barking in the distant yards. I left a card with a poem "Introductions" in Da. Ml.'s mailbox. Had he not said to me that he was a romantic I might be more afraid of his response, but I can't be worrying about it now.

I'll let fate do its own thing. Oh I wish he could sneak away tonight and show up at the rehearsal but I know that's impossible. The show that he's seeing will probably go on much longer than we'll be rehearsing. Still . . . I long to hold him in my arms and be swept up by him again.

Saturday: Went to the armory to rehearse part II. Da. Ml. and I kissed passionately in the W.C. He said he was busy and could not get together in the afternoon between rehearsals. However, he showed up as I was finishing my sword fight rehearsal. I went to his house and we made love. We were going to wait but after lulling about for a bit we just gave in. It's been very long for me, lying down with a man. It took my usual time for me to get my head on straight (pun intended). And to think that tomorrow is our "slipper brunch" at the house! *Quelle folie* !

Sunday: The slipper brunch . . . A great success! People seemed quite impressed, not that that was the point, but that they all enjoyed themselves. The pot "treats" were a *big* hit. Everyone got quite blottoed within the hour. The good vibe between the cast members was especially nice towards more and more bonding. There was talk about forming a rep company of some kind once this show closes! Da. Ml. was there in all his beautiful self. I'm still at a loss for words when I see him. Saw *Year of Living Dangerously*.

Journal – March 6th, 1983

I hope I make some sense of this. I'm very stoned as I try to jot this down. We just had our "slipper-brunch party." Total success. Everyone seemed to be having a good time. It was exciting to see people happy with the show's progress and with the people they're working with. That's always a plus . . .

. . . It's much later as I enter the rest of this entry. Da. Ml. called. He said something really sweet to me and I can't wait to see him tomorrow. I wonder if he'll like the book.

I also spoke for a while to Monsieur back in New York City. What an interesting time this is. He was best man at St. Le.'s wedding. I'm so happy for St. He always wanted that "special someone." I have no real notion of what I'm doing with this new liaison. Its potential power is just beginning to dawn on me. When I sense that Da. Ml.'s responsiveness is as committed as mine, then I'll have a big decision to make.

The Week of *March 7th – 13th*

Monday: Well nothing in my wildest dreams would have led me to believe I could be involved in this kind of a production, playing Romeo in *Romeo & Juliet*, having this liaison with someone like Da. Ml. Nothing! My time is spent living between the moments when I will be seeing him next. And even though I lie with Coo, my heart rests with Da. Ml. at this point. Nothing will make the next while an easy time of it for any of us.

Journal – March 7th, 1983

I'll be fit to be tied very soon. My enamored self, whose sole purpose these days is to be with, to touch and to make love to Da. Ml., is going berserk. Of course he has to work, meet his commitments and continue his life so why am I so upset at not being able to be with him at present?

If only I could be certain of where his affections lie, how deep his yearnings for me really are, then I might be more at peace with myself. But as I write I haven't got that knowledge, only hunches as to his heart's commitment. Though I will survive this, I want much more than the little of what I've just tasted recently. Oh, Da. Ml., read my thoughts, make me yours for as long as we can.

Tuesday: Slept in and then took care of co-op ad customers. Rehearsed with A. Buresch, and then Coo and I went to AAA to sign up for the services. I sent in my *R. & J.* ad for Backstage back in NYC. Rehearsals went well. I feel ready and on top of things. It can only get better, right? No?

Journal – March 8th, 1983

Oh Da. Ml., if I were younger I'd surely write these words to you and send them via a beautiful card, never doubting the course of such an action, but I'm 28 and I'm a married man and I've loved and been loved and somewhere along the way I learned that it was not always necessary nor wise to do so. Yet, if you but gave me my cue, I would be yours forever. One word, one sign, one action and I am more than yours.

Wednesday: Of course it's an affair that I'm having. The entire day was filled with relentless guilt at feeling that it was over as man and wife for Coo and me. Facing her is so difficult now. After rehearsing with other principals at A. Buresch's, I went over to Da. Ml.'s. We spoke a lot. He told me about himself. With this love, this passion, I begin to feel a new sense of strength. Oh, that I had a confidant around here with whom I could pass all of this by. Equity contracts finally came through, and our picture with a promo for the show was in the local paper.

Journal – March 9th, 1983

Shakespeare's lines permeate my own; their wisdom, along with their sharp rebuke, tear at me. My passion for Da. Ml. surpasses anything from my past, if only because I'm old enough to know better. But I can no more control the stupidity of its intensity or my compulsive behavior to want him for my own than to stop breathing. I'm sure all the books advise other tactics, counsel moderation, but that is a word I'm no kin to. The simple idea of that word—moderation—bores me to tears. With moderation comes boredom, roots too sturdy to ever be rocked, where only conservatism can grow.

Still, the agony of doubts regarding reciprocity gnaws at my sanity. For the heart and soul are fed on hope . . .

Journal – March 9th, cont'd

Amidst the confusion, we mustn't mistake the few pleasant lulls between the storms for a change in weather. The weather remains the same and only a drastic move to another place could maneuver the impasse to a more temperate climate.

Thursday: Dropped my motorbike off at Honda shop. Met Da. Ml. with Bb. at the theatre, and got started with some of the sets. Of course at night I was bummed out when Da. Ml. said no to me to coming over to his place. There is so little I can do to make that man fall in love with me like I am with him. Why are the inequities of falling in love with men always so bittersweet?

Friday: Each day is as intense as the other. My highs are as dangerous as my lows. I'm at the complete mercy of Da. Ml. and his feelings/lack of them for me. Met him early for breakfast at his place. He had to leave for a business breakfast. Sound familiar? Too familiar. Spent all day working on sets. We spoke briefly about living together. Ironic that I'd want monogamy with him! It's certainly all fire for now. So intense, the pain is felt in every part of my body. Worked a full day.

Saturday: Up early to work some more on our sets. Left with Da. Ml. around 5:30 to go over to J. & D. Marg. Met an older gay couple there, St. and Ji. Went back to Da. Ml.'s. In the midst of lovemaking he let me know quite gently that he was definitely not in love with me. Even if you know it, even hearing it, it doesn't compute with one's senses, which seem on a one-way collision course of their own. I still will stay with thee and never from this palace of half-light will I depart, till thou requests me to!

Sunday: Things are just beginning here. Worked in the AM on moving the set into the theatre. Left for home to work on taxes and get some rest. Did a tech with cue-to-cue for lights and sound. I'd love to bed down both D. Rob., *and* A. Buresch. I'm so out of control here, aren't I?! Let's hope I don't act on any of these desires.

Journal – March 13th, 1983

It's midday and I have important news as to this precarious love story. Yesterday, after working all day on the sets and not having gone over to Da. Ml.'s place the night before, he asked me over in the evening. We were settling down to lovemaking after a lull in the preliminaries, when I mentioned my love for him, or rather my being in love with him. That's when he told me that this wasn't the case for him, nor could it be so, he thought.

My heart swelled but I managed to muffle the sting. I lay by his side and withheld my tears as best I could. I thanked him for his honesty. He clarified what he meant by saying it was respect for me. He said he felt the love, could perhaps learn to fall and be in love, but for now, he did not have to offer the all-consuming passion I had for him.

If only we could control the folly of our love, perhaps then, the heart would stand a better chance at survival, perhaps that small, articulate piece of flesh could escape the senseless miseries that love's confusion often prescribes. For once in love are you a step closer to being out of it.

It strikes me as too bittersweet, how we spend our lives in the to and fro from lovers' houses, seeking asylum in the niche of those pendulums. Such dreaming that goes on there! Why must we wake from them, as though lost in a cold back alley, having to reconstruct our paths to sunnier streets, find new avenues in order to start knocking on more doors? How redundant, this foolish pain!

Journal – March 13th cont'd.

We did a tech run of the show followed by a cue-to-cue. It's so nice to be in a dressing room again. Even if the pay sucks! The people really are a great bunch and though my jealousy for Da. Ml.'s attention is strong, I manage to control it remarkably well.

The Week of
March 14th – 20th

Monday: Slept in till 1:30 PM. I needed the rest. Picked up my motorbike and took it for a ride up to A. Buresch's, and then to Da. Ml.'s. He wasn't home. It was nice to be on it again. Both the bike and car are costing us so much money in upkeep. Rehearsals went so-so. Had hassles with dressing room space. Bb. and I had a small tiff over lighting and acting problems. What can I do? Da. Ml. sat in my car tonight while we chitchatted and it took everything on my part not to ravage him.

Tuesday: Time is flying by and soon we'll be in front of people. Did errands and a tech dress rehearsal at night. It wasn't bad. Went down to Albuquerque.

Wednesday: Some of the cast members and I did publicity stunts at the Plaza, the State Capital and La Fonda. It was okay, if a bit nerve-racking. We did three-quarters of a run in the afternoon. At night, met Da. Ml. for a soak. I feel the bond between us tighten and I only want it tighter. The whole cast of *Don't Drink the Water* was at the Soak. It was a classic Marx Brothers routine. Just as I was about to walk into the restaurant from our spa treatment, the door opened and Da. Ml. pushed me right back into the back part of the place. He managed to sneak me out by the staff exit. Worked on costume and props till almost 2 AM. Got ripped on ash oils.

Thursday: Opened in *Romeo and Juliet*. I was tense since I'd not been in front of an audience in a long time but I persevered. Sadly, I went up on my lines a few times but overall there was a good feeling about the endeavor. I could have killed Bb. for doing some touch-up painting of the balcony without telling me! Both fights went badly but, apparently, the audience didn't pick up on any of that. Cast party was great. We all drank fine champagne courtesy of Joe. Da. Ml. was sloshed on his cold meds. I wanted to hug him—he was so adorably cute. Doug asked me why I didn't come down to say hello to the cast last night at the Soak. I denied ever being there!

Friday: Slept away the day. At night, I hurt myself during the sword fight with Tybalt. I busted cartilage between rib and sternum. I went on for the last part of the play with the help of a shot of morphine thanks to our resident physician. I managed okay; then I went with him to the emergency room after the show. A surgeon friend of his gave me a shot under the rib, which hurt my lung. I was out cold on Valium and barely managed to say goodbye to Coo in the early morning when she left to drive out to Los Angeles.

Journal – March 18th, 1983

Life works its mysterious ways . . . Second night calm worked well for me but not so for some of the other cast members. Mi. especially seemed to be stalling for time to find his lines. At the end of Act One I hurt myself somewhere during the sword fight and ended up with a fractured joint at the juncture between rib and sternum. I let Pl. give me a shot of morphine to get me through the rest of the play. That did the trick. I wasn't affected as far as the acting went but I did feel a slight buzz.

I went to the hospital afterwards and a doctor friend of Pl.'s took care of me. The treatment, however, seemed a bit worse than the pain from the accident. I'll just have to persevere. This, on the night before Coo leaves in the very early morning for her LA sojourn and I prepare for my liaison with Da. Ml. to go into full swing. I can't help but follow through with what feels right to me. My love for him grows daily, and each day sees me falling deeper and deeper.

Saturday: Slept in. Da. Ml. came over with soup and some chicken. He snuck into bed with me. Then we went over to the house where he's housesitting and I slept some more. At night, our Paris had no voice, our Juliet had been in a car accident and I needed two shots of morphine just to go on! And yet, it was an excellent show! Afterwards, I went over to Da. Ml.'s and we made love . . . sort of . . . with only mild success at penetration on his part. His cock is not the easiest thing to slide into me.

Journal – March 19th, 1983

It's past midnight and I'm at home, which feels empty without Coo's presence. I just spoke to Se. who was too stoned to talk. That miffed me. He could have made an effort, no? I'm waiting for Da. Ml. to pick me up. And though I know he will, my past experience with Monsieur always leaves me with nagging doubt.

Why do we run from the surest loves of our lives into the riskier uncertainty of new and lustier loves? Even if I can sit here and feel certain of Da. Ml. on some level, why do I feel jealousy as to his whereabouts and with whom he might be with?! He's forewarned me. I know him for what he is. It's that degree of noncommitment that brings on these unhealthy doubts.

> *What a day! Playing Romeo with ruptured cartilage in my ribs, shot up on morphine; Coo leaving for a month to Los Angeles; Da. Ml. ready to deflower me as soon as I say the word . . . Will I live to tell <u>that</u> tale!? We hope so.*

Sunday: Woke up to Da. Ml.'s amorous energy and we made love frenetically. I just love being with him. Sound familiar?! And from lessons learned, I try to keep *some* emotional distance. He brought me home and I did a mailing to various LORT theatres. At night, unsure if he was picking me up, I walked to see *Skin*. It was a lousy show, too self-indulgent, but a good experiment on their part. We grabbed a bite to eat and then came home. I orgasmed by fucking him; a first for me, I believe. Coo called. Also spoke with Se. in Toronto. A week, too full for words, comes to an end.

The Week of March 21st – 27th

Monday: Woolf's quote about having to put order to her ideas rings familiar. Woke up late after the phone kept ringing on and off. Didn't do half of what I'd intended. Sent off mail to various contacts. Spoke to a lady in the post office who had seen the show. I "bipped" around town on my motorbike. Did a taping of two scenes for local cable TV. Da. Ml. came over for supper. Went over to Ralph Levy's to watch scenes from our play, then a movie. Slept over at Da. Ml.'s. Finally had slightly better success at anal sex. I'm confused but happy. The pain in my chest from the fight sequence is quite unbearable at times.

Tuesday: Interesting that the nights I sleep in my own bed are the ones I tend to forget to enter. Dropped off negatives at print place, cashed check and went to library. I bumped into To. Ga. and looked at his artwork he had in his portfolio. Some beautiful pieces, excellent concepts. At night, we had a run-through. Can't recall who drove me there. Spoke with Mk. Pa. It's strange sleeping alone. Went out for ice cream with Da. Ml. and we dropped by his office afterwards.

Journal – March 22nd, 1983

All this life is just one colossal experiment towards no real conclusions other than the one big certainty. It's towards that end I vacillate through life's intangibles, trying to rescue any hidden reality from it, truths that have a way of escaping us more times than not. Amidst my newfound freedom of living alone and for myself, I dream of adventure and success.

My amorous feelings for Da. Ml. are tapered by the reality of my marriage. It's that slow awakening from love's feverish pitch as I try to fathom the long way home, not quite remembering how I managed to get there to begin with. His smile, his liking me, and yes his concern for me are like a nest where my heart finds nourishment and rest.

Now for the more serious task of writing and tackling From Now On *towards fruitful completion.*

Wednesday: Up early to work at the co-op. It went well considering I'm doing the tasks of two people while Coo is gone. Dropped by the newspaper and got leads for ads. I'm anxious to see my article in print. Did banking and bought film festival tickets. Bought *Life in the Theatre* and some undershirts. Came home to messages from everyone. I'm so happy when Da. Ml. calls me. The review came out. The worst crap I've ever read. Spoke with Coo. Saw *Sophie's Choice*. Da. Ml. met me and I spent the night over there. No lovemaking, though I did manage to come. We read *Life* and *Treats*. Slept in wonderful peace.

Thursday: Da. Ml. dropped me off at the print place. The prints didn't turn out that great. Got a call from Coo. She came close to getting a part in a production of *Women Behind Bars*. Da. Ml. dropped by but I wasn't ready nor was I dressed to go out to look for music. A. Buresch picked me up along with Mk. Pa. At night I imposed myself on Da. Ml. and stayed over there. The morphine shots are playing a strange game with my psyche, I think . . . ?

Journal – March 24th, 1983

Why must the hours of night be so short when you're in love? Why do we let ourselves fall asleep, missing out on that time when we could be holding on to each other more tightly?

Yesterday's local review was abysmally cruel. I have never had any critic be so crass with regards to my stature. I wonder how badly this will affect ticket sales?

Saw Sophie's Choice *last night. Everything in it had an effect on me, the fact that he was a writer, Sophie herself, their love, its intensity, the Nazis . . . And here I am, enthralled in the raptures of love, knowing full well that Da. Ml. need only ask me to love him fully and completely and I would.*

Where would that leave me and Coo? Where indeed! Her letters/cards arrive every day yet my guilt diminishes with each one for I've made up my mind and nothing, it appears, will change it. If I'm not strong enough we will never accomplish this end to our marriage, and I mean to accomplish our split and maintain the friendship at all costs. I have to. I know it can be done.

As for my writing . . . well, no progress there. As soon as the show closes I'll regroup and see what comes next. As for Da. Ml.'s show, who knows? My chances of getting a part appear to be 50/50 at best, but then, what more can I ask for than even odds? Lots, but I can't so I won't.

Friday: A productive day given the weather, my state of health and my schedule. Da. Ml. drove me home around 1 PM. I wrote a bit, slept, read, and ate. The show was good but not many people in the house. Opted not to get any morphine tonight. After the show, I grabbed a bite with A. Buresch, Za. and Da. Ml. He drove me home afterwards and came in, then decided to ask me to come over just to sleep. I'm sure it's because I can't/won't be able to do so for a little while.

Journal – March 25th, 1983

Is love so cruel? Da. Ml. asked me stay over at his

place last night and I agreed, though I knew full well that he wanted to be alone. I know that I could handle that sort of dynamic once I had a commitment from him, but now, at this early stage, it just confuses me.

The nightly shots of morphine are like a poison dragging me into its slow abyss of deceit. It seems to say, yes you can do it alone, but it's much more fun and a lot easier with me along for the ride. Cunt! Cunt! I will not give in to your suggestive powers. I'll endure my pain because I'm strong enough to do that. I won't use you unless I feel it's absolutely unbearable to go on stage; that the pain will take away from my performance, my capacity to perform.

In this late morning of a god-awful day, with snow lulling in a thick gray cloud just over the mountains, I sit here with the possibilities of A. Buresch moving in with me for a few days. I'm trying to foresee all that that might encompass. The complications could be huge . . . But maybe Da. Ml. would be happy that I was out of his hair, out of his way for a bit? His words on the phone a little while ago were cold, distant and curt—in a way that I'm beginning to see is his approach to not being hurt by all of this.

Here I'm offering everything that I have and he's unsure . . .

Why must people reject the love that's offered them? Or is it more that men do that, gay men more so than straight men? They always want the other one, where they feel like they're the chaser not the chased . . .

Oh sun, trying so damn hard to peek past the carpeted sky, try harder, for your warmth is needed now, needed badly. I woke up today in some nightmare where I was biting a nose, an ear and a toe off of someone who was trying to prevent me from continuing my journey on my motorbike. Is that a sign! Am I now on the verge of physical combat? If so, who am I going to bite, who is it that I'm going to attack?

Saturday: Stayed in trying to handle the onset of another cold. Da. Ml. drove me home around 11AM. I was so tired. I slept and rested for our last show. We had a few more people than the last two nights, but still it was quite a difficult crowd. Had a shot of morphine for the last act. At the closing night party I ate ash oils, smoked Thai stick and drank too much. Da. Ml. had shaved off his beard by the time he got to the gathering. I didn't even recognize him! I suddenly felt very guilty being stoned, though *why* was beyond me. His aloofness along with his cold words as we left the party totally confused me. What am I trying to pursue here?!

Sunday: The week comes to an end with drinks and a light supper at Da. Ml.'s with To. Ga. and A. Buresch joining us. We had this heated discussion about artistic integrity. It's hard to swallow that crap after struggling for so many years. At least Da. Ml. and I saw eye to eye on this. It made me love him even more.

Journal – March 27th, 1983

The show is over. When was the last time I worked at this time of year? I think it was when I did Quadrille *at Lincoln Center, unless I was doing the* Mute Girl *shoot around this time last year? I can't recall . . . The void that I feel is rather phony. I can't be dishonest and deny the fact that being alone now is a greatly appreciated luxury. It permitted me to experience the play more fully along with all the mix of relationships the show brought.*

But Da. Ml., his whole attitude, is affecting my mood. He's shaved off his beard. He looks crueler and more severe without his Friar Lawrence whiskers, like someone I don't really know all of a sudden. It's starting to dawn on me how little we do know each other. Anyone can talk about themselves but until you experience them firsthand, how they are and how they react to various situations, it's hard to fathom that. I just hope he trusts me enough to open up more to me.

The Week of
March 28th – April 3rd

Monday: Hard time getting up. Dropped off tapes at TV 6 and met with Carr. only to be told of a loss after expenses were paid off. Shopped and prepped for the Seder. It went great, not too much Hebrew, but fun nonetheless. Nice people. Pl.'s kids are just beautiful. Came home and spoke to both Mk. Pa. and A. Buresch. Da. Ml. came over afterwards. I can tell he's quietly contemplating if an "us" could manage somehow. Spoke with Monsieur briefly.

Tuesday: Did errands. Picked up tapes of two scenes and dropped one off at Da. Ml.'s office. Ralph Levy was there. Couldn't decide if there was any meaning to his wink, if he suspects our affair or not. Spoke to our neighbor across the way, who said she enjoyed the show. Worked at co-op and then Da. Ml. picked me up and I spent the night over there. We finally managed to succeed, more or less, with anal sex, but I have no enjoyment from the act at all, even if my orgasm *was* incredible. Umm . . . ?

Wednesday: Woke up from my drugged Valium sleep. Early morning sex was unsuccessful for me but good for him. We went up to see the ruins and the top of this volcanic mountain. Both were so different from each other and yet that close in proximity. I gave him head and came while in one of the pueblo caves. Got back home and dozed off. Went out to ABS and indulged myself. Watched a part of *The Ritz*. Spoke to Nl. out in LA. I may go out to surprise Coo. Talked with Da. Ml. around midnight. He thought I was coming over. Oops.

Thursday: All the days weave together, one with the other. Did some ad rep work in the morning. Went out for lunch at Na. & El. Ma.'s. Interesting time, though I noticed today how set they are in their ways. Came home on the bike through heavy winds that could have been a tornado, they were that strong. Sleep falls into my eyes like sand on my eyelids and nothing can wake me at times. Talked with Mk. Pa. He's horny and lonely. Saw *Siberiade*. I loved the epic quality to it all. Drove bike over to Da. Ml.'s. Snuck into the darkened house and into his bed. Both of his arms had fallen asleep under his weight!

Journal – March 31ˢᵗ, 1983

A few lines to tell a tale that's ended. No more avenues can open up for Da. Ml. and myself. It seems we were a part of each other's lives but we don't have what it takes to become a couple. My life with Coo is perhaps not over? I know that her love for me is awesome but too much for me to reciprocate. Our future talks will have to deal with it as it comes, in as best a way as possible. Now, for our careers to hopefully continue and progress.

Friday: Up early-ish. Made love, Da. Ml.'s way. It's our last time in that house-sitting space, unfortunately. I got an invitation for supper to St. and Ji.'s for next Wednesday. That should prove interesting. Hung about for a spell, then drove my bike around the foothills on my way home. Na. Ma. called to say they'd hated *Siberiade*. Went to the bank but it was closed so I couldn't pay the electric bill. Who knew! Had lunch with Mk. Pa. He played a great April Fool's joke on me. Cleaned up the house at night and then over to Da. Ml.'s place. Once Coo returns, all we'll have is friendship. That's all, just friendship.

Saturday: Got back home around 11AM and got ready for my audition. I showed up only to discover that Tom Gartner had to go out of town. He'd left me a note with the office manager at the theatre, so I went back home and waited for Da. Ml. to show up. We went to see photo exhibit at Hoshur Gallery and then dropped off audition material for *Craters*. Can you believe it, here I am advertising for my own competition! Had a lovely Italian meal and saw *The Meaning of Life*. Enjoyed it. Came home and to bed alone. Alone, alone, with a lovely wife far away and a cherished lover much closer and yet just as far away.

> *Journal – April 2ⁿᵈ, 1983*
>
> *Where will I be when I return from Los Angeles, without Da. Ml.'s affection, that very real physical contact? Yes, I'll have his affection as a friend who cares for me but will I be able to see him around town without going crazy from the lack of our touching? Worse than that, will I be able to hide my true feelings from Coo?*
>
> *All these complications in such short periods of time. How lucky will the next bit of future be for us? Da. Ml., how far away are you really from me? I have no way of knowing. Have you ever given yourself up to anyone? Is that why you're so reticent in giving yourself up to me?*

Sunday: Went to K.K.'s to see the video of the show. I guess I'll buy a copy. Went over to J. Go.'s for brunch. We were about 7 or 8 of us. Mk. Pa. finally left to go to his uncle and I stayed amidst mostly strangers. J.J. told me she wanted me to do *Ah Wilderness* for her. Somehow, though, I just felt uncomfortable. I left there and came home. Da. Ml. had returned my gloves with a note so I went over to his place. We made love and he fucked me successfully for the very first time. The pain, though, continues to be just unbearable and excruciating. It was more like getting aped. If that's how it feels, then I'd just as soon take a pass on it. We spoke of us living together.

The Week of
April 4th – 10th

Monday: A lousy day, weather-wise. Stayed in and wrote. Did laundry and general clean up. Spoke with Da. Ml. at least 10 times. Spoke with Coo and with Nl. At night, Mk. Pa. came over and slept here. I had meant to not get involved, but who's kidding who! Well . . . why not, I mean, why not!

> *Journal – April 4th, 1983*
>
> *Well—out of nowhere—Da. Ml. began to talk to me about "us" and the possibilities of living together, that is, if/when Coo and I were to break up. He was clear that he would not be part of any broken marriage. That's his rule. So where does that leave me? When I speak to Coo on the phone I get that old familiar feeling of being relaxed and totally understood by someone.*
>
> *Da. Ml. put it rather aptly yesterday when he said my decision was to choose between two precious stones, a diamond and a pearl. So very true . . . My love for Coo is more boundless than I realize and I know once she's really gone from my life, that's when I'll miss her even more. But the harsh reality is that I've lost that commitment to her as a husband. As friends, I want to be able to continue the friendship and be as close as circumstances permit. However, the reality of breakups rarely permits that kind of relationship to grow, certainly not at the very beginning.*

I'll be going out to Los Angeles and once there, I'll try to make up my mind. Even now, my love for Da. Ml. is evolving. The lust is mellowed out, mostly because of our very different sexual proclivities. I got fucked today—or rather last night—for the very first time and the pain was immense. I think I may have actually thrown out my chest from the experiment! Whatever happened to the good old days of simple "frottage"? Gone, gone, gone . . . Now's the time, I guess, for all good boys to grow up into men. Do I want to—that's the eternal question.

Tuesday: The sun was finally shining as Mk. Pa. and I woke up. I went off on the bike without my helmet and froze to death. Paid bills and went around doing some shopping, some errands. Rewrote last chapter of *Cooperative Murder*. I decided they needed to get caught in the end. Da. Ml. came by in the afternoon to pick up headphones. He was *so* amorous, so unlike himself. It's day and night all of a sudden. I know that I'm pushing my orgasms out there! Spoke to Coo for quite a while at night. Went to see *The Outsiders*.

Journal – April 5th, 1983

My body begins its slow-paced, self-destructive journey. In typical overdone fashion, my profligate sexuality traipses its diabolical urges along, only to have me collapse exhausted, injured and spent from giving in to them.

From the arms of one to the arms of another, I lose sense of all that I know is right, leaving me to deal with the after-effects that always surfaces from this complete abandon. I find myself forcing out orgasms like an extortionist with inner demons, pushing with unnatural might whatever bit of dead sperm that's left, tucked away inside the canals of my scrotum. Complicated by others' affection for me, I'm unable to refuse. Da. Ml., why have you all of a sudden become so engrossed with me? Have your feelings been hidden even from yourself up till now?

I find it hard to decipher the emotional growth that appears to have taken place within the span of just these last few days. Why did I not foresee this potential complication before it reached such proportions?

And Mk. Pa. are you satisfied? What more can you expect from this friendship? Will it leave you feeling more superior or will it pass, be simply water under our bridge? As usual, time will weave its ultimate tale with this one.

Wednesday: Another day in hibernation. Why bother venturing forth when the weather out there seems to belong to another season altogether! Da. Ml. picked me up for supper at St. & Ji.'s. Clive, a friend from Berkeley, was very charming. Excellent meal, lovely wines. Went to Da. Ml.'s for the night. We read a play from his NYC partner, quite a good mystery. But he was antsy and was not into being touched. He got quite defensive when I started analyzing him. He did *not* like that at all. I had a hard time falling asleep due to all the food and drink I'd consumed.

Thursday: I'm a pitiful basket case. Woke up with a hangover and before I knew it, I was away from Da. Ml.'s, back home, and he was off to breakfast with his ex, Steven. That fucking name yet again. A nemesis for life! Slept the morning away. Did errands in the afternoon. Had an ad rep meeting and got lots of new leads for sales. Mk. Pa. dropped over for a bite. At night, Da. Ml. came over with his friend and we got stoned on ash oils that his friend was selling. I guess I needed it. Da. Ml. called me later on when I was *very* stoned. He read me some of his material. Excellent stuff, just excellent. I called him back to tell him as much. I feel cold and hurt and yes, a little jealous.

Journal – April 7th, 1983

What's there to be said that hasn't been said before! Sleeping over at Da. Ml.'s, without even touching, leaves me feeling blinded by a saddened rage. If this is a time-limited affair, we have lost yet another night to take advantage of each other's company. The passion that I seek is not uniquely sexual, though that aspect is certainly a close second, but it's the love and its incumbent passions that I seek.

In less than a week I return to my wife, and in so doing, I confiscate your love. In doing so, I tear away at my heart, and the bleeding—contrary to what you may believe—will not cease overnight. The trickling drops will gather inside of me, converge in my chest, my head, down to my very soul, and I can assure you that it will be agonizing. I don't ask any questions because I know the answers by now.

> *And that pain begins, all the same, for the knowledge predestines my actions. Even as I write I can feel those first drops . . .*

Friday: An easy day, trying to get as many ads done over the phone. Did my S.F. Festival Theatre audition and got a callback. U.I. called me. There is no record of my new case! Dropped off fact sheets for ads. Made supper for Da. Ml. Then he left and I went to the Gala opening of Film Festival, klieg lights and all. Liked *One from the Heart* a lot. Came home and then foolishly drove my bike all the way up to Da. Ml.'s. Froze to death in the process.

Saturday: Up early, made love quickly and then split. Got ready to go and see *Our Hitler*. I didn't make it past 2 hours. Came home, wrote and rested. Did a Chinese supper in the wok. Dropped by ABS before going to the Armory to see *The People*. It was a lousy print. Na. & El. Ma. left early. Met a lovely girl from Telluride. Came home and watched TV. Called Coo. Spoke to Da. Ml. and wrote "In Pursuit of Love: An Answer."

Sunday: I have cards coming out of my ass here. The week ends on a hopeful note. Two callbacks should establish both of our futures for the next little while. Getting both would be excellent, even one would be sublime. As usual though, all it is for now is hope. Saw four movies today. *Grey Fox* had folks in it that I'd worked with back in Canada. Mild success here would surely translate into more work for me up there, right? Had an ugly little quarrel with Da.

Ml. We patched it up but our time's clock is running out. Strange this world we live in.

The Week of
April 11ᵗʰ – 17ᵗʰ

Monday: It was a busy day doing errands. Helped Mk. Pa. with an audition piece for this British theatre program being set up in town. Went to the VD clinic to try and sell some ad space. Missed the first part of Oscar broadcast due to wrong listing in the TV Guide. At night, Da. Ml. was quite out of it and not open to any suggestions, and yet, he's always kind in some way or another. At least he's honest. Or am I just a sucker for this punishment?

Tuesday: Busy day. Made love to Da. Ml. and came home ready to face the challenges. Ad rep meeting with client went okay. Mail brought in a chain letter. Great, just what I needed on a day when I have two auditions— one of them a callback, and a land lottery selection. The Festival Theatre audition went well. It's between me and David Marshall Grant. Yeah, like *that's* going to happen! My *Craters* audition was the pits. Who's doing me any favors here?! Da. Ml. called late at night to tell me I hadn't gotten the part of Tom, but that it looked really good for Coo. They want me to stage manage and have Da. Ml. as my assistant s.m. Is that wise?

Journal – April 12th, 1983

Is this the second or third ending I speak of, as it concerns my affair with Da. Ml.? He was antsy today, full of too much food and liquor and was not in the mood to be touched. Again! His words telling me "there was no magic for him" and "that if I left Coo, not to come to him," were sharp, clear, and painful. As I lay beside him—holding back my tears—when he got upset and told me to stop it, I wondered again at how much he could possibly have loved in the past. If it's presumptuous on my part, it's only because I found his impatience so cruel.

Yet in the morning as he succumbed to morning testosterone I was glad that this love, this friendship he says he has for me permitted me to orgasm with him once again. This foolish trip into that magical valley where only love supposedly blooms!

Journal – April 12th, later on

I just love the weight of this journal, the way it looks and feels in my hands.

A strange day that's still not over. I met some lovely people at one of my advertising contacts, a school for alternative studies. I left there to go to my audition for Tom Gartner. I thought it went well. He said it's between me and David Marshall Grant. Yeah . . . ? Right! Taking him at his word certainly makes me feel good but I doubt that DMG won't be available to work in the very theatre he supposedly suggested be created in the first place! Maybe this audition will help me further down the road in my career . . . ? What a dream come true it would be to do that show sandwiched between shows right before and right after with Madeleine Kahn and Richard Chamberlain respectively.

Then to go from that to my audition for Craters *where it was over before I even knew I'd done it. I'm feeling the usual empty, cold, awful feeling of not even being in the running for the damn roles.*

I'm now stoned as I look around trying to evaluate my life and its recent goings on. I haven't a clue as to my future. Reading through the 15th anniversary issue of New York Magazine, *I just know I don't want to go back there at all, not for quite a long time, not unless the perfect package appeared, not unless it was for a conquering experience. Wouldn't want to repeat the struggles from my five years in <u>that</u> city!*

Journal – April 12th, yet again . . .

Long day, with three entries. Count'em, three! Da. Ml. just called. I can't play the role of Tom. I'm not right for it according to his colleagues. Not the right . . . energy? Or the balls . . . to pull it off? Apparently my height was an issue. I don't like this at all. Like the NY magazine article said, "if not this one, maybe the next?"

Wednesday: Okay, day number two with this plan. Ran errands and tried getting together what needed to be done. Went for a swim, only to have the place filled with kids so I left. I picked up a sound effects tape and redid outgoing message on machine. Da. Ml. came over at night and we chatted. He reiterated their offer of stage management. It's only for four weeks on a guest artist contract, but I would be getting a per diem when I was in Los Angeles. I read him some of my material from *From Now On*. He said he loved it. Gave him a card with a poem.

Thursday: Emotional day. Mk. Pa. came over for breakfast. Then I packed and Da. Ml. picked me up and took me out for a quick bite for lunch before dropping me off to catch the airport shuttle. No great emotional goodbyes. I touched his knee briefly and got no response. Once in Los Angeles, I met Nl. He wasn't at all what I'd imagined. Or course, Coo was blown away by my being there. The expression on her face was unbelievable. We made love and got stoned. Shopped for clothes and went to Canter's and up in the hills for a scenic overview of new hope . . . perhaps?

Friday: Up early to go and visit "Disneyland." Hard to imagine that *this* could be a dream come true at my age!! We were too tired at night to do anything but crash.

Saturday: Went out to the beach at Venice. We saw Sn.'s car there. It seems he lied to Nl. and Coo. Poor Nl. How I could empathize with him, but of course I couldn't say so. Bought a new Walkman and some sex toys and some tapes. Spoke at length with Nl. at night.

Sunday: Up at 4:30 AM to leave Los Angeles. How do I feel? It's hard to say. With enough money, I certainly could enjoy Los Angeles, but even then, only for short periods of time. Still, I get a sense that this is where I need to be heading. We drove all day. Ate and smoked grass and arrived home safe and sound. Can't wait to find out what auditions we have from Albuquerque agent, and how *Craters* will take shape for Coo. If I can just get lucky with Festival Theatre! Or any other stuff I've auditioned for!

The Week of
April 18th – 24th

Monday: I'm back home and Da. Ml.'s voice is what wakes me up. Why is life so complicated?! I guess I'll be stage managing *Craters* . . . as I pursue happiness in other ways while trying to take responsibility to not hurt those I love and with whom I've made a commitment. Still, that dream of escape and a life on my own stays vividly with me. Saw a lot of people today. Wanted the day's audition to be so good and it turned into rat shit. Tried to write a bit.

> *Journal – April 18th, 1983*
>
> *I'm trying so hard to read all the signs to understand their messages before the shit hits the fan. My surprise journey to Los Angeles was successful in many ways. However, I couldn't discuss anything with Coo other than a future together as opposed to one apart. I was thrown off kilter by the power of my own feelings for her when I saw her standing there in front of me. Our time together was well spent, I thought.*
>
> *But now, back in this Santa Fe environment, not even one day into the routine, and I'm not enjoying it. My sense of my own self is somehow diminished and I feel cheated in my own space, my own life. All the pluses and minuses need to be added up and figured out before anything more can be done.*

> *The fact that Da. Ml. called around 8:30 AM and said something as endearing as "he'd always take care of me" didn't help matters any. Oh T., les complications.*

Tuesday: Trying to settle back into some kind of routine here. Tried to write. Read more of *Harold*. Spoke to Da. Ml. (more on that in my journal). Went swimming at noontime and then to ABS. Worked at co-op and saw *Chilly Scenes of Winter*. Not bad. Could obviously relate, and yet I was left feeling empty. Came home and made new outgoing tape. Got stoned.

Wednesday: Spoke to Da. Ml. and Monsieur, all in the same night. Can I take this?! Here I am, having just skimmed some of my 1976 diary entries with those memories of freshly stirred pain, and I'm telling Monsieur about Da. Ml. while he's telling me about Eric and their relationship being over. He completely ignored my remark about us "just having to get back together again." Stayed up late to watch movie. Can't wait to see Da. Ml. tomorrow.

Journal – April 20th, 1983

Nothing seems to be better. I have lost it. But I know that I can't have the other thing, this love for someone else who doesn't love me. Reading through my diary pages of 1976, I realize how fucking insane I was, in what I went through with Monsieur. And here I am, it seems, at it again. Now, however, I'm wearing both sets of shoes. I am Monsieur to Coo's me, and I am me to Da. Ml.'s Monsieur. Oh those two roles we play in this world that we live in, the one who loves and the one who is loved.

Thursday: Da. Ml. came over for brunch. I explained to him how I still felt. He kept his distance but managed to show me some affection. He left behind his backpack and just as he came back and knocked on the door, I was jerking off and coming at that same second. Now *that's* timing! Went swimming at night, and then over to ABS. Met Thad. Seems like good fling material. Writing *From Now* On very steadily.

Journal – April 21ˢᵗ, 1983

La maladie, la maladie, encore la maladie . . .

Da. Ml. dropped by for lunch and here I am, once again, in the throws of love's obsession. He is as beautiful, as sexy and as inviting as ever. But as I've been told already, I cannot have him. Not even if I were single and unattached.

God this is terrible. Do I need to continue in this complicated state of affairs, knowing full well the agony that awaits me? "How oft when men are at the point of death have they been merry . . . "!

Irony would have it that he left the house but forgot his knapsack and I was on the brink of orgasm when he returned for it. He kept knocking so loudly on our door. I had no choice but to tell him exactly what had transpired. That got him smiling. I should have told him how "good" he was, or rather had "just been," but didn't think of it till later! I would so love to have the chance to play house with him. I wonder if I ever will?!

Friday: Wrote in the morning. Da. Ml. called to tell me the show was being postponed till late May. I guess it's okay. Went out to Cerrillos with Coo. Saw movie at night. Got home to a nasty message from Mk. Pa. who was upset because he thought I'd told Da. Ml. some things about him. We settled the confusion after much wasted time arguing over it.

Saturday: Da. Ml. called and picked me up around one. We went over to Tm. Ml.'s place to be interviewed for the job of houseboy/companion. The timing would be perfect now. I repeated my usual plight to Da. Ml. but to no avail. He has such a wonderful smile. We went walking downtown and bumped into Thad. Took a bike ride at night, feeling very restless. Did Coo's hair. So much for excitement!

Journal – April 23rd, 1983

I'm going crazy. To be more specific, stir crazy. I know that I'm such a cruel bastard but I would like nothing more than to be with Da. Ml. That's right, Da., I'd give anything. I know that I can't go over there. He'd just be upset and wouldn't deal well with me at all. He'd just send me packing.

So I sit here, idly biding my time till fate loosens the noose and hangs me or sets me free.

Sunday: Up early to see antiques show. Then we drove out of town to see some homes and possible land sites. I then took it upon myself to try and drive all the way up to the ski basin on my motorbike. What an exhilarating experience to get to that kind of elevation. Went out for coffee and desert with Coo and Da. Ml. at La Paloma at night.

The Week of
April 25th – May 1st

Monday: Lousy way to start up the week. Looked at apartments. Feh! U.I. is such a massive fuck-up. No one has any idea of what's going on with my case. I managed to do some writing. Didn't get the job as houseboy/caretaker but I did set up an interview for the landscape gardening assistant position. At night Coo and I went to food shop. Da. Ml. surprised us and invited us both over to a friend of his.

Tuesday: The days get worse, not better. A long day of sorts. We went to do our co-op work. Then I had a hassle with this doctor for my asthma medication prescription. Two interviews for handyman/garden work got me two temp jobs. So here we are back to the grind. Came home and wrote some more on *From Now On*. Late in the afternoon we went to an open house, not bad at all. I so wish we had that kind of money. Saw *Bad Boys*. Great performance. Grabbed a bite with Mk. Pa. Back home now and feeling in limbo. What's next? Surprise me, universe!

Wednesday: Went to work as a gardener's assistant at the Seldon's. Five full hours of hard labor for a salary I wouldn't even offer to a lame workhorse. But it's honest work *and* it's legal. At night, I went to see Da. Ml. at the latest house where he's housesitting. Had a heavy tête-à-tête with the usual outcome. What will time do for us I wonder?

Journal – April 27th, 1983

Well, this journal should be entitled "Life Without Da. Ml." Son-of-a-bitch, even his initials send me in a state.

It hurt even more tonight than ever before. When he told me he'd done it with this eighteen-year-old and this other guy it was reminiscent of so much of what went down between Monsieur and me. God, how I could have hurt him and yet . . . I could never do something like that.

He is more adamant than ever that nothing can take place between us. Even if I left Coo and I appeared on his doorstep two years later. He loves me but isn't in love with me. Point finale! So what do I do to go on living and forget about him, about us? He seems to think that that's a simple thing to do. I don't.

What I felt when Coo first went off to LA is very much what I still feel inside me. It's in a less intense focus perhaps but I don't know if it's not even stronger now. The longer I live with the idea of a split, the easier it becomes for me. Unfortunately the only danger is that it will come as a catastrophic blow to Coo. Is fate going to be kind and help us through this with some good fortune? I wonder . . .

Thursday: Worked for Rad. in the morning. Such hard work for so little pay. Found out I didn't get the other gardener job that was going to be for the next few weeks. For the better? Tried to write. Rep meeting was quick. Tape was sent back from Stratford in Ct. Got stoned at night and took a walk around town. Beautiful weather.

Friday: Oh Da. Ml., you hurt me so much more than you realize. Doctor's appointment went okay. Did a lot of sales calls. Had lunch with Mk. Pa. and did errands with Coo. At night she went out with Da. Ml. to see *Throne of Blood*, then out for a bite with him. It seems he's leaving for a week in Phoenix. I'm glad I know about it now. It reminds me of the time he left during rehearsals for *R. & J*. I just know he's going to fuck around when he's out there. Oh love, I hate the very sound of your name right now. You're killing me.

Journal – April 29th, 1983

The days are too short, the life over with too quickly. I'm sitting here in my office around 7:20 PM. The spring sun outside my window is glorious. I can see it's slowly setting in the distance. Coo is out with Da. Ml. and I'm home trying to write. Got monies back from A. Buresch. There is no tension between Coo and myself but there exists this unspoken thing. Lives are meant to be lived; we help each other out as best we can.

Journal – April 29th, later on . . .

Oh Da. Ml., why can't I just stop imagining you fucking with all those friends of yours? Those images *should tear away at any romantic notions that I have for you. That boyish smile of yours is really just a killer in disguise, isn't it! How <u>do you</u> go about your seductions? What was it in you that demanded I grow up when the part of me you seemed to like best was my youthfulness! Did you resent that in me because your inner child had died/was dying/is dying as I write?*

What was it that I heard today? You can't lose a love unless you found them in the first place . . . . ? Did we ever find each other, truly find each other? I don't know. I thought I had, I thought we had.

Saturday: Momentous day. It was five years ago today that I escaped to these United States. I worked all day as a gardener. Finally decided the time had come for me to speak to Coo about our lives and my wishes for a legal separation once we moved out to LA. It was difficult. She was *so* emotional and I felt so cold and withdrawn in response to it. We took a walk around downtown and got stoned. Will we be able to navigate around this one? Keep it civilized with some degree of finesse to the friendship? I hope so.

Sunday: Got up to tension and another heavy discussion, reiterating the same arguments from last night. I left to go swimming, and then over to ABS. I went to this guy's house for a quickie. Went to Mk. Pa.'s workplace. His coworker gave me this book called *Letting Go*. Came home and Coo wasn't there. My original thought was correct; she'd gone over to Da. Ml.'s. Supposedly she didn't discuss anything with him concerning us. I wonder if he wants to see us stay together as a couple?! Things do seem a bit calmer now. Still, didn't I do this once before, in November of 1975!?

Journal – May 1ˢᵗ, 1983

During the last 24 hours my life has taken on the newest meaning it's had in some time. I finally spoke up and told Coo I wanted some kind of trial separation. I feel so cold and removed from it all. I can't help it. What's been forming at the back of my mind is now a fact for her, a seed that must be planted and permitted to grow in her psyche.

I have no clear picture of the future. I just hope for the best, and wonder how this next month will be, living together in this house before she leaves for LA to rehearse the show. Before we know it, the next step of our lives will be here, in another place, another space.

It's just 5 PM and I have no idea where she went and in what condition she's in or how stoned she is. I just hope she didn't call Da. Ml. for a shoulder to cry on. Talk about the complications <u>that</u> would entail!

The Week of May 2ⁿᵈ – May 8ᵗʰ

Monday: The days are simply here, and there is so little to them . . . We are in a silent limbo, awaiting the eventual trial and tribulations of our move to Los Angeles and a final separation. Mail brings little. It snowed while I was slaving away as a gardener so my hours were shortened.

Came home and did some writing. Refrained from calling Da. Ml. We went out with Pl., his wife and some friends of theirs. Had a nice time. We got stoned later at night.

Tuesday: Up early to do senior citizen work at the co-op. Did some errands and then wasted both time and monies at ABS. Home to finish the *Story of Harold*, and other materials. Spoke to Da. Ml. briefly. Saw *Flashdance*, no plot but great escapism. Got a letter from Stacy now in NYC, and spoke briefly to Chri. back east, and the night is not over yet. The mention of moving seems to bring a lull to our various moods. Read parts of 1977 diary—it sounded so chaotic, more than I remembered for that year.

Wednesday: Worked a full day for Rad. There was a hot Spanish number at J. Sic.'s house when I knocked for gardening supplies. Shouldn't it have been the other way around! Saw *The Hunger*. Loved the movie if not necessarily the story.

Thursday: A day to myself, sort of . . . Had audition for commercials. Feh! Did errands. Took a walk in downtown core. Felt very sexual so I dropped into ABS. Bumped into M. Sto. in the place!! Then I had this encounter with this hot black stud named Bill and threw caution to the wind with that one. Got stoned at night. We got word that *Craters* is definitely on. Co. Mi. called from NYC. Also found out that A. Buresch may be coming back from Austria.

Friday: As usual, I'm not entering as regularly as I would like. Worked a long, hard day for Rad. My hands are feeling worse and worse from all this manual labor. I dislike the grittiness of the job but I enjoy being outside, facing the assorted landscaping challenges. Finished reading *A Boy's*

Own Story. Can relate to some of the material, but didn't like the ending.

Saturday: Another hard day, worked till 4:30. Met D. Pars.' lover. Great looking guy. Dropped book off at Da. Ml.'s place in the morning. He was on the phone and I had to get to work so we didn't talk. He dropped off the script at the house later on. God, how will I survive this! The thought of watching someone else play the role of Tom while I have to stage-manage makes me cringe. What I do for bucks! Saw *The Hostage* at night, not bad. Met Linda who's playing the Virgin Mother in *Craters*. Went to Da. Ml.'s for a snack!!

Sunday: Left for Taos. Great ride but not so great a town. We got ripped and stopped to watch a boat race down the Rio Grande. Had such great views, listening to music on the headphones. Came home and crashed. Night spent watching trash TV but at least we got to bed early enough for a change.

The Week of
May 9th – 15th

Monday: Another week, ugh! At night, Coo and I read the play and made a list of her possible props. Tech guy from *R. & J.* came over for us to sample some dope and ended up getting very ripped. Coo and I had an intense discussion. She can't see the end to our relationship. Sound familiar!? It concluded on a fairly positive note thanks to us being *so* stoned. Read her some of my poetry but I had to skip so much of it because it centered on being in love with someone else.

> ### Journal – May 9th, 1983
>
> The word standstill scares me because it's self-inflicted. The new situation we find ourselves in reminds me of our own responsibilities in this lifeplan of ours. These days, Coo and I live surrounded by the unspoken presence of pain and heartbreak, along with dashes of confusion. We are together but I find it difficult to show affection towards her for fear of fueling the wrong fires.
>
> Our friendship is one that I desperately need but it gets confused when the wife/husband aspects get involved. I wonder how we'll survive the proposed outcome I've outlined.
>
> As for Da. Ml., there is only the nostalgia of what once was/could have been that touches me. I'm only slightly hesitant at what might happen as I tackle the stage management job for his company's production of Craters, knowing that it's just like riding a bike and that I'll pull off the gig without any glitches. I'll remember all the little things that need to be done for me to do a decent job of it.
>
> I'm stuck a bit with From Now On because I need to do some more social services research to move the storyline forward.

Tuesday: A very long day. Seven and a half hours of manual labor and mostly nonstop. I felt the crunch on my body.

Late at night I just lost all of my energy and felt almost ill. Saw *Time Stands Still*. Didn't do much else.

Wednesday: Oy vey. The show is now postponed till August! Trying to decide what to do. Perhaps it's for the better in that something else may come around for me in the interim. The in-laws will still be coming out at the end of August as planned and we're still scheduled to move to LA some time in September. Worked for a few hours of landscaping in the morning, then dealt with advertising sales for the remainder of the day. Met the set and tech directors for *Craters* and managed to put my foot in my mouth with the producers this afternoon. Really, who cares! It's not like I'm a full-time stage manager worried about losing gigs from this. Waiting for Se. to call from Toronto.

Thursday: Worked a full day. Having to deal with the workers who are tearing down the present storage and greenhouse on the site is a bit tedious. Dreams of fame and fortune help me pass the time of day and permit me to escape the drudgery. Se.'s call last night made me feel so much better. Seeing Da. Ml. in the early mornings doesn't really help, does it!

Friday: Saw Da. Ml. again before going to work. How confusing for the cerebral heart. Worked a three-hour day at landscaping. Then I went about doing errands, picking up ad copy for the co-op paper. Bought gardening supplies and redid some of the garden space in the back and side yards of our house. Our friendly supplier brought over some grass and hash. Got stoned. Went to the library on my bike, then Coo and I moved me over to the house for my weekend of housesitting. We said goodbye rather quickly. Did a lot of reading. Mk. Pa. came over and we went to ABS and then to the Soak for a bite. On our return, there was a power failure. It felt scary to be in a strange house on Friday the 13th with all the lights out.

> *Journal – May 13th, 1983*
>
> *Housesitting in this exquisite adobe for the weekend, a few minutes after Coo left, and here I go snooping to find "les accoutrements des accoutrements"! My immediate reaction: shock. Not from any sense of prudishness, but more from simple ignorance about this type of paraphernalia. And to think that I thought I knew Da. Ml. I <u>should</u> have known better. People are either all there, out and open, or they just aren't. I'm beginning to wonder about other markers on his body . . . on the arms, and his lower backside. Is it really a skin condition or all a cover for his kinky sex life?! Deception, deception . . .*

Saturday: Got up and went about getting ready for workday. I can't emphasize enough the luxury of this wonderful place. Worked six hours, but it wasn't too difficult. Raking new-mowed lawn does get to be tedious though after a while. Rad. and D., the sculptor, got stoned at lunch break. That surprised me. I left them around 3 PM and bought food at the deli. Did some reading, some writing, and watched TV. I'm still spooked by Da. Ml.'s sexual proclivities, and upset by it too, that I didn't know it before this.

Sunday: My weekend retreat comes to an end. Had a nice time on my own. Coo dropped by mid-afternoon. I could sense my reticence on seeing her and I knew that she sensed it, too. Did a lot of writing on *From Now On*. At night, ate grass and hash, and saw *Local Hero*. Liked the film a lot.

Came home and planted indoor garden start up, as well as repotted our pot plants. I hope they last.

> ### Journal – May 15th, 1983
>
> The weekend is practically over with. The luxury of this adobe has come to an end. Got some good writing done, some escapism, and now it's back to the realities of my life.
>
> If we had more money, I mean tons of it, would I accept different terms for us? Would I simply disappear now and again to form liaisons, or would I insist on divorcing, permitting me the chance to connect with a male soul mate if that was in the cards for me?
>
> This early mid-Sunday, wearing an old familiar cologne from Da. Ml.'s cache of bottles, makes me recollect my Montreal days rather vividly. Is this entire Santa Fe situation simply a repeat of that era, especially now that I'm about to stage-manage just as I was back in that town? Will September bring a love of my life all over again, the way Monsieur showed up on that Labour Day Weekend, my first upon moving to Toronto? A decade later and a decade wiser? How perfect that would be.

The Week of May 16th – 22nd

Monday: No work so I tried to accomplish a lot, but a lot of time was wasted just running around for nothing. We taped this one woman from the library to help Coo with her accent for *Craters*. I'd started to compose a letter to Mrs. F. when out of nowhere, D. Farber called. He apologized to me and said he'd made a mistake. It was encouraging to know that I was right all along in my convictions about how fucked up Direct Centering was.

Tuesday: We're getting stoned too easily these days. Watched *Playing for Time*, a powerful piece of documenting. Acting was superb. When the Jews came out of the camps and forests at the time of liberation, it was as if they oozed out of the woodwork. Did only five hours of landscaping work. Spoke briefly with Da. Ml.

Wednesday: All these days that are breezing by us so swiftly. I tried to write mid-day after running some morning errands. Went to the ABS in late afternoon. Dropped by Da. Ml.'s and went over to his landlord's house. Such a beautiful place. I read him some more of *From Now On*. Lying next to him gave me some much needed security. When he teased me with that elastic to my tits, I could tell that he knew that I knew what he's into with his other partners! I just hope he doesn't give me that option! He's still so beautiful to me that I might not be able to resist that offer. Saw *Moonlighting*. Not as impressed as I thought I would be.

Journal – May 18th, 1983

The fact that love is an addiction doesn't help matters much. As with any other addiction, we will lie, cheat and deceive ourselves to try and get just one more "hit" from our engulfing passions.

Thursday: It's Sunday as I write stuff down. Worked a full day shoveling dirt and weeds so that finally we could begin to do some planting. Got stoned at night and watched trash TV.

Friday: Another long day at work, 8½ hours to be exact, painting lawn furniture for most of it. Dropped by Da. Ml.'s and had one of our heavy encounters. Strange, that at first, he didn't try to answer the door, as though someone might have been there with him. It's the same issue as always: he just doesn't feel for me what I feel for him. Coo's existence had nothing to do with our demise! My pain over this is so strong. Of course, he called at night to see how I was doing!

Journal – May 20th, 1983

The more times I hear him say it the easier it will be to leave Da. Ml. behind. He is such a kind individual. I've never met anyone like him. In many ways he may not have what it takes to be a lover to me, though I continue to believe that it's more the physical thing with my not being able to fuck him and my not being into kinky sex. It's interesting how things can go one way and we'll be very close and all of a sudden he decides we are getting too close. It's so hard to deal with the hot and cold thing.

At least he's kind enough once he's rejected me, or rather, told me how it really is, to make sure I'm okay. Of course, he continues to repeat that there's no magic there for him and he should know. He says he's not even looking for love anymore and that Coo had nothing to do with he and I not having a successful relationship.

Well, we'll be leaving Santa Fe soon enough and I guess I'll be leaving him behind with it. The friendship will, with any luck, remain, but as we know from past experience, friendships with old flames are a challenge to maintain.

Saturday: I left early to drive to Albuquerque for my photo session. They were running late. The photographer seemed pretty good. Now, to see the results. Went to the ABS down there and got it on with my usual type. Da. Ml. called at night. He'd gone to see *Local Hero* and hated it. Figures. He told me about a dream of his but I had a hard time staying focused on all the details in order to figure any of it out. Saw these incredible townhouses in Albuquerque but I still can't believe the exorbitant prices they're asking. They're just not worth that kind of money. Went to bed early feeling a bit under the weather.

Sunday: Our agent woke me up with info on another audition so I had no choice but to get ready and drive back down to Albuquerque again. The damn thing was just a cattle call, but the ad agency seemed encouraging so . . . who knows?

Journal – May 22nd, 1983

I need to read, Letting Go *a lot more than I care to admit. I will not be okay with Da. Ml. till I have moved away from this town. Of that, I'm quite certain. Not till I'm living on my own and have possibly met someone else will I be able to get out from this funk.*

I should count myself lucky that I'm capable of writing anything down. This bug that I have these days is a constant worry. Too much pot? Hepatitis? Mono? AIDS!? This death wish is so permanent an institution it's difficult to fathom anything coming from my pen other than suicide notes. I want to write down how shitty I feel not having Da. Ml.'s love reciprocated. How absolutely horrendous the sensation is, that he has none of the feelings for me that I have for him. How utterly cruel and unfair it is, the agony of one-sided love on the sane mind, this having to endure, mostly in silence, the erosion of a burned out, crushed heart.

The Week of May 23rd – 29th

Monday: Worked a full day but it wasn't too excruciating. At night I decided to go swimming and of course Ge. was there. The timing was finally on our side and we managed to have our cars pull up together at the corner after the swim. One thing led to another and he and I went over to Da. Ml.'s small place. We got ripped on hash and got to know each other a bit better. Lovemaking was okay but nothing to write home about. He said this was his lucky day!

Tuesday: Our house is slowly entering a state of confusing emotions. We are in pre-mourning stages for Ms. K.'s untimely demise tomorrow. Shed tears for her life; she will be missed. And yet, even out of this chaos, Ge. and I managed to meet up. He came over at night while Coo was out. I was happy to see him at the pool and even happier to have him come over.

Wednesday: A day off. Ge. came over. Had an okay time. It's funny to see him so aloof about sex. If there was ever one thing in life that I've never been aloof about, it's sex! My lusts and passions have never had any bounds. I only managed to write a bit today. At night, I ended up going to bed early. Our days here are strange. We are no longer man and wife. The gap widens and much is lost into those crevices. We brought Ms. K. to the pound for her last snooze. It's a sad, sad thing to have lived such a stress-filled life only to die now from feline leukemia at such a young age.

Thursday: Ms. K. met her maker early this morning. Those strange, frightened bright yellow eyes no longer look out onto this crazy world of ours. I worked all day at landscaping. At night I went off riding on my motorbike and gave in to seeing Ge. at the pool. We went to the Soak. It was a little boring. It's frightening how little in common we have. Decided not to get together tomorrow. Dropped in at the ABS. Feh!

Friday: Worked all day at gardening. Not too difficult but it's manual labor nonetheless. Spoke briefly to Rog. who seems more aloof then ever. Ironic that he knows

B.J. from C. Palermo back in Little Italy. Small world. At night, I got stoned and watched *Sound of Music*. Such easy habits. A time to work, a time to play . . . but when do I write?

Journal – May 27th, 1983

If I persist in writing the account of my life it's because I see a sense of accomplishment as my annual diaries and my years-long journals pile up. These journal addendums to my diaries are the best footnotes I could have asked for. I wonder if I'll ever tackle the job of transcribing the decade's worth of work thus far.

These last days have been filled with a new sense of euphoria. Having finally gone to bed with Ge., the diver from the local pool, I can write about what it was like, where once it was all just speculation. That we actually managed to get together at all was a feat in itself. His shyness and my married state made it almost impossible to connect. Still, time and the fates were on our side.

The sex was okay but lacking. When I think about my own burning desires at his age. He didn't know I was married until after we'd had sex. That proved awkward! He seemed genuine when he said that he, too, had been fantasizing about me. However, if I recall correctly, the reality of a teen's dreams when they come true are often quite disappointing.

I wish I could have spent the night with him but that was impossible for the both of us. Me to a wife and he to his parents! In three visits we made love only twice and

> *then on our fourth get-together, when he had reservations, I spoke up and he admitted that he wanted some space. By all means, have your space.*
>
> *My heart fluttered a bit, but my mind, being quite unchallenged with the encounters, had no arguments whatsoever. Though we may see each other again, I doubt it will be possible to carry on like this. Even if it was only once in a blue moon, I can't see an easy solution for these trysts to continue.*

Saturday: A long tedious, strenuous day of toiling and tilling the land—picked and shoveled all day long. Rog. left with a mere wave of his hand after just a few hours. At night, I almost called up Ge., but resisted the impulse. I got stoned instead on some leaves from our pot plants. Not bad. Coo went out with Da. Ml. to a movie and then to a jazz pianist concert. I was out cold. No writing done at all.

> *Journal – May 28th, 1983*
>
> *Just a little bit stoned. I tried some of the grass we've been growing and I think it may be a winner. Let's hope we get some seeds out of this. It would be so nice if I could be productive and write while under the influence but it's too difficult for me to sustain any cogent line of thinking when stoned. And of course, now, in this state, I so doubt I'll ever amount to much with this writing of mine.*

Sunday: Another long day of gardening but at least it was at home and for us this time. Coo and I then went over to Mk. Pa.'s sister's graduation party later in the day. At night we had a moment of tension when Ge. called to invite me to his place. I had no idea what to do. When I did go, of course two of his friends would show up unexpectedly! With me standing there beside him, he outed himself to them as bisexual. I do sense an attachment growing but he, too, will be leaving town to go out of state to university. He'll be gone, a thing of the past.

The Week of
May 30th – June 5th

Monday: Most of my nights are spent stoned and exhausted and consequently I have no energy to write about its contents. Saw Ge. at night for our last time. Saying goodbye was quick and thereby painless, with the lovemaking session having all the trappings of young love/sex. Memories of a time gone by for me . . .

> *Journal – May 30th, 1983*
>
> *The days are such that I feed into my melancholy and none the wiser for it, I remain the fool. Youth is such a tantalizing thing. It evokes neither love nor lust within me, just a naïve curiosity. I pursue its magic trying to remember perhaps its passage from my life?*

How peculiar that I cannot remember being in my teens, just as it was not so very long ago, or ever having left them. How different am I, was I, from this Ge.? As I get to know him better I realize that his initial silences were somewhat deceptive. He appears to know the score quite well indeed.

Sadly, nothing I can do or say will make things any easier for him. I can only be honest and treat him well. This bird will soon fly away and the hand that felt that rapturous beating of his young heart will be just that, a hand, if a bit heavier from the experience of having known his touch.

Tuesday: The day off was a much needed break. I did a lot of ad sales pitches but with only so-so success. Started to buy more garden and yard supplies for the house. The design is slowly taking shape out there. Did some writing. Da. Ml. came over for tea.

Journal – May 31ˢᵗ, 1983

I said goodbye to Ge. last night. Perhaps it's for the better that he's leaving now. It will make it easier in the long run. However, for the record, the attachment was there, if purely from my end, a combination of love/lust for who he is. I may see him again by chance when he's back in town, but for us it's over with. The irony is that I really don't have a clue how he feels about it, he says so very little. Life goes on as usual . . . or does it?

Wednesday: Worked a full day at landscaping. Had some hassles with 8 X 10 negatives. Our headshots can't be done the way we've been getting ours done back in NYC. I'm ready to give up on all of it! Bought hair clippers. Saw *Return of the Jedi*.

Thursday: I had my morning free to do ad rep work. Co. Mi. called from NYC. Worked landscaping in the afternoon till five. Did I go crazy today? I cut my own hair! There are days when this existence leaves much to be desired. Went with Da. Ml. and Coo to the carnival. Spent money on nothing. And of course, Da. Ml. would hate rides.

Friday: A long, full day at the salt mines. No mail, no calls. I did however get my pay raise. I guess I should be ecstatic, but $4.50/hr ain't nothin to celebrate! Picked up garden supplies and then took a bike ride in the late night and dropped in at ABS. What else is new!

Saturday: Another full day of labor, only to follow it with a trek up into the mountains with Coo to find flagstones and small tree specimens. We came home, planted and planned and then planted some more. Got a call from agent for Monday auditions. Yippee. Got our contact sheets back. There were some okay shots. Called home to see if Mom and Dad would be coming out to see us but they've decided not to. Oh well . . .

Sunday: Slept in. Went to look for more stones up in the mountains. At night, got really depressed watching the Tony's. It's an almost impossible goal, isn't it?! But at least our move to LA is a change in the right direction. I must keep believing in that. At night, Coo, Mk. Pa. and I went dancing at Zorro's. Of course, old pangs awaken. That familiar world of knowing what's there and what isn't, it still manages to mesmerize. What a life!

Journal – June 5th/6th, 1983

Just watched the Tony's. It's so difficult to accept that hint of defeat connected with our leaving New York City. I know myself well enough to acknowledge that, had we chosen to stay on, nothing but a lost life existed there for me; and probably for Coo as well. So here we are, estranged in the land of enchantment.

My gayness beckons and I need to answer its call. If unhappiness lies ahead it's no different than what I've already experienced in life and survived. In a world filled with so many signs that something big awaits us, I can't lie back and accept anything but that, something big to happen. And I will get it.

The Week of
June 6th – 12th

Monday: A full day. Did ad rep stuff in the early morning and then drove down to Albuquerque for auditions. They went okay, I guess. Came back to Santa Fe to do work at Seldon's. When I was finished and got into my car, I saw a note from Da. Ml. asking me to go over so I did. The usual chemistry for me, and today he was in a friendly mood. The old cat and mouse routine of power and submission, or do I just read that into what we have going on between us? Home, TV, ABS. The same old shit. Wrote a letter to D. Farber.

Tuesday: Long day's journey into nothing. Workdays just get done and I come home too exhausted to write. No acting, nothing but mild depression. My visits to the ABS should put me into their top ten best customer list, surely.

Wednesday: What did I do? I worked a long, strenuous day and came home to find out I'd gotten the role of the Chinaman in that tacky spot for local furniture chain. I just sense how awful it will be. But when ya gotta, ya gotta, and *I's* gotta!

Thursday: The day was an incredible experience going down the white water rapids of the Rio Grande. My body aches all over but such a sense of accomplishment. We had this great guide, Scott. At night, Da. Ml. and I went to his spa, and then saw Za. at dessert shop. We went back to his office and had the usual session of his teasing me on and my not being able to resist. He of course then reverts to cold, cool, calm and detached. This is sick, Da. Ml.

Friday: The days whisk by. Heavy work all day long. Dead tired, I came home to find out Coo and I were having Chinese dinner with Da. Ml. and a friend of his. Had an okay time but afterwards I asked him to take Coo to this party but he couldn't. A faux pas on my part, I'm afraid. He's out presently, probably fucking his friend, so I can't call to make amends. Guests at the Seldon's asked me to sing some more when they overheard me singing by myself from their window!

Saturday: A very long day, struggling to survive it all. Worked for Rad. at the Seldon's, getting the place ready for their party. A lot to do with not enough time to do it in. I left at 5:30 whether he liked it or not. At night, I went swimming and to the ABS. Came home and eventually to bed.

Sunday: Up early to ready myself for the commercial shoot. It wasn't as bad as I expected. The tech part was okay but my makeup was simply dreadful. I still can't believe the pay I did this for, or the total release I signed away. Went to the ABS down there and had a nice encounter with this guy from Santa Fe. Then I went up the Sandia Peak Tram and got stoned at the top of the mountain. I practically saw god, it was that awesome! The wind was blowing so badly as the sun began to set that they had to delay the tram service for a while. Being under my Walkman didn't hurt the atmosphere either.

The Week of June 13th – 19th

Monday: Slept in until Coo woke me up to inform me that two huskies were camped outside our door. Rick's dogs had managed to escape and find their own way home! Did errands for ad work and then home to write a letter to A. Buresch. At night I went to see *Eating Raoul* with Da. Ml. Not very good. Ah lost love, gone, gone gone . . .

Journal – June 13ᵗʰ, 1983

A brief entry about Da. Ml. Though I know it doesn't work for us, that it can't and never will, there is something I'm unwilling to lose when it comes to him. It's not just the love or simple attraction; it's something that goes deeper.

I find him so beautiful.

Tuesday: Called Se. at night and chatted away. He saw Monsieur at the Stratford Gala who proceeded to inform him of what went wrong between us. It was my extremes. Nah, ya think!

Journal – June 14ᵗʰ, 1983

Before I know it I'll be living in Los Angeles. How ready am I for that! As ready as I'll ever be . . . ? Hard to say.

These days feel like tiny footnotes to my life.

I just got off the phone from speaking with Se. I really love that soul; he's the closest to my embryonic self. It's the whole French Canadian identity reflected back at me. He saw Monsieur at the Stratford Gala and they had yet another of their "talks" about me. Monsieur told him that what caused us to separate were the extremes in my personality. I can certainly buy that.

What can I do? It's not something that I necessarily dislike in myself.

I can't wait for the next big change in my life. I can only add that I'm happy to feel that I'm in control of this new step.

Wednesday: Had my discussion with Rad. about too many hours and how I'd like to quit. I don't think it sank in, though.

Thursday: All the days seem to repeat themselves here. No writing can be achieved when my hands are too swollen to write with. I picked up the rest of the flagstone and a few more trees. Got stoned.

Friday: I feel like some poor impoverished child at the turn of the century, the work is *that* hard. The hours are too long and I can barely manage to live through to the next day. I went to swim at night but the pool was closed. Had a lousy time at the ABS. I missed out on a potentially great encounter but it was just taking too much time to get the connection going.

Saturday: Worked till 2:30, came home and then went out to get my hair dyed blond. At night I saw *Body and Soul* with Coo, Mk. Pa., and Da. Ml. An interesting movie. We went out for a bite and then home exhausted.

Sunday: We slept in. I tried to do a few things later on in the day but it was useless, I was too exhausted for words.

The Week of
June 20th – 26th

Monday: Worked all day at landscaping and came home for lunch only to find a phone message from swimmer Ge. The rest of the day was spent trying to get in touch with him. We finally got together late at night and made love by the riverbank. Pleasant, *if* risky. I wish I hadn't already gone to the ABS and had a steamy encounter there prior to our meeting up. I've got an audition tomorrow for a national commercial. Monsieur called. It was nice to hear his voice.

Tuesday: The audition was a waste of my time. I didn't even get on tape. I could have killed the agent for even bothering with this submission. I was *completely* wrong for the call. Came home and went to do my landscaping job.

Wednesday: I was back on the job today when I got another audition for tomorrow at the R. Johnson agency. Rad. flipped out and fired me on the spot. Hallelujah! Did core work at the co-op and came home. Had time now to do some work on our own yard. The design is coming along.

Thursday: Went down to Albuquerque for the audition. It went well. I could certainly use the bucks. Went to the ABS down there and had this encounter with this blond, aging hippie. Had a great time. Came home and did a few errands. Planted a few new things in the yard and finished the patio layout. We bought a gorgeous desk at the antique show. How foolish are we here!? The in-laws arrive tomorrow. Gulp.

Friday: It's so nice to see them again. They are the salt of the earth. We drove back to Santa Fe and went out for a quick ride about town, then off to supper at a Japanese restaurant. We bumped into Da. Ml.'s dinner companion from a few weeks ago. He didn't say a word to us. The in-laws didn't accept our monies. We picked up our desk along with an antique necklace for Coo.

Saturday: We got up early to go out to Los Cerrilos. After a lovely morning there we came home to watch the video of *R. & J.* Drove them around town a bit more to give them a better idea of the area, before going out to the artist's foundry in Tesuque. At night, we saw *Blithe Spirit*, not bad. Saw Bb. and Carr. at the show. Bb. is *such* a lovely fellow.

Sunday: Went out to Bandelier National Monument Park to see the black mesa and visit the pueblo. Came back and took a nap before supper. Went out to see *The Survivors* at night.

Jan. 1st, in Acapulco

Jan. 5th, before the sofas arrived

Jan. 26th, with N. Mainville and Rrrocky

Jan. 28th, gift of ink drawing by N. Mainville

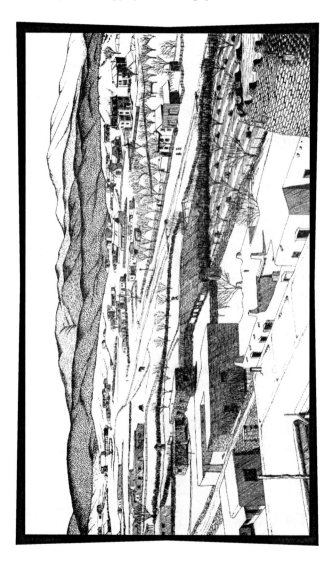

March 15th, R. & J. tech run

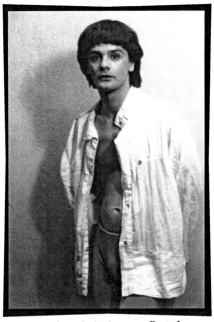

March 25th, backstage in R. & J.

March 26th, Da. Ml. without his beard

April 17th, card cover

April 17, 1983

My dearest husband,
    These are; "Merry Christmas, Happy Hanuka, Happy Anniversary, Happy Birthday, Happy Valentine's Day and Happy Easter/Passover", presents. They were bought with love and not too much of our dwindling fortune.
    I've said it before and you'll hear me say it again but I thank you for your support and encouragement throughout this whole experience, and I offer you the same anytime you feel the need for your own future adventure.
    I want us to be together through all changes. I want us to be strong individually and together. I want us to share more adventures in our lives.
    My love for you grows as my love for myself increases. Both are the foundation on which my life is built.
    I remain devoted to you......

        your wife
        your lover
        your friend
            Coo ♡

April 17th, card from Coo

June 9th, whitewater rafting on the Rio Grande

Aug. 1st, Monsieur at his cottage

Aug. 17th, postcard cover

Aug. 17th, postcard from Coo

Sept. 2nd, at the Mainville's

Nov. 24th, Coo with Mk. Pa. at Thanksgiving

Dec. 24th, Christmas in LA

Cover from the author's 1983 diary

The Week of
June 27ᵗʰ – July 3ʳᵈ

Monday: We shopped at Jackalope and spent time at the Museum. Ate lunch at the Soak, then walked up Canyon Road to window shop. A possible encounter at WC in La Fonda made me decide on a trip to the ABS. Had an encounter but no entertainment! Back at the house, Mr. C. gave me an auto mechanics lesson. We stayed in for a quiet evening.

> *Journal – June 27ᵗʰ, 1983*
>
> *These times we live in, to what purpose are we enlisted? What great scheme are we bound to? Or is it that most of us aren't bound to anything? And only a few, through sheer will, deep-rooted in need, make bold attempts to make their mark, one they hope that stands out. That need for fame or infamy . . . I wonder if anything comes from such obsessions. Do I care what my words create? I think I do.*

Tuesday: Back to being a writer more full-time now. Slept in before tackling some rewrites. Pl. dropped by to pick up the videos. Went to Gooch's luncheon. It was okay. There was a great entertainer, B. Hall Jones. Did errands with Coo. Bought a typewriter and did co-op work. At night I couldn't go for a swim but managed to score at the ABS. These are the initials of my life here!

Wednesday: A lazy day of typing and trying to write. Did some work out on the yard. Tried to go for a swim but the pool was too crowded. Had an encounter at the WC in the downtown library.

Thursday: Coo was fired today. A blessing in disguise? Went to see B. Hall Jones at La Fonda and went out dancing at Zorro's afterwards. Tried to get in touch with Da. Ml. to let him know that I didn't want to stage-manage their show now that they've changed the gig from a five-week to a crazier four-week contract once again.

> *Journal – June 30th/July 1st, 1983*
>
> *Is this to be a repeat of my Montreal days, gay clubs and all?*
>
> *Dancing away in the one gay establishment in town reminds me of so many other places, so many other towns. But this place is too small for it to feel comfortable.*

Friday: Went over to Da. Ml., and informed him of my decision. He seemed to take it rather well. Anyway, the director has his own stage manager that he likes to use, so it's all for the best in the end. Found out that Hope Lange is no longer doing the show. At night our landlord came over and said he liked the work we'd done so far on his property. We drove out to catch the last act of the opening opera for the season and stayed for the gala. Danced Viennese waltzes under the stars. We went out for a bite later on and bumped into Carlos and this other man who was with him.

Saturday: Slept in. Did a few errands and then to the ABS, not once but twice today! A bit too much here, don't you think?! At night we got stoned and went dancing at Zorro's. T. Gartner was there with David Marshall Grant. Well . . . at least we looked presentable! I wonder if I ever had a chance at that part?

Sunday: Slept in till almost noon. Just a lazy day of resting up. My foot felt mildly sprained so I tried not to move it too much. Not much typing, just enough to keep me vested as a writer. Saw *Betrayal*. Excellent piece of theatre, executed so well.

Journal – July 3rd, 1983

I am not stage-managing for Da. Ml.'s company. No matter what kind of pseudo-Catholic guilt tries to usurp this newfound sense of well being, I won't give in to it.

It's all for the better. Ten years ago this August I joined Actors Equity Association as an assistant stage manager. I don't think it's any way to celebrate my life by relieving that experience. Something else will come my way. I know it.

The Week of
July 4th – 10th

Monday: Happy fourth! This is my fifth year in the U.S. of A. Up very early to have breakfast with Na. & El. Ma. up on Canyon Rd. Decided to dye my hair red for the occasion and ate some grass, then we went out to see the fireworks. We followed that by going to this live "happening" up on Gonzales Rd., thanks to Carlos's invitation. It was quite trippy with a lot more people than we expected. Came home early.

> *Journal – July 4th, 1983*
>
> *Poetry, with that great passion to live, is a young man's profession. By that definition it must be brief, right?*

Tuesday: Slept in again. Met Ge. for lunch and then I took him up to Da. Ml.'s to make love. It was okay. At least we know each other and have a sense of what to expect now. Did some typing and sold some ad space in the latter part of the afternoon. At night I met Da. Ml. for coffee. We had a very good talk. Dropped in at the ABS and went over to this guy's house for a very quick quickie. I didn't even come but I did indulge in poppers. He had such an incredible space.

Journal – July 5th, 1983

Courting AIDS is all I can do to describe my life's habits. Need I say more!

Wednesday: Encounters like these don't happen very often. I went to the ABS and hit pay dirt with this guy Victor. What can I say—he was a blond version of Monsieur's old *Godspell* fling, Ra. On. It was spectacular. We spent I don't know how much time in this one booth and ended up sweating like pigs. It must have looked so comical as we came out of there. Of course I did everything I shouldn't have done. I licked his sweat, even swallowed some of his cum, something I've never voluntarily done hardly ever before!

Journal – July 6th, 1983

All these entries! This is a continuation of my diary entry. I took a walk with Victor and we covered many topics. He's pleasant enough . . .

Hard to decide what else could be there. What I do know is the body. What a hunk! But he's so much taller than me. I had that distinct crick in my neck from looking up.

Looking forward to the near future.

Thursday: Had a few ad sales meetings. I'm just typing

away and trying to keep fit. Getting stoned at night does not help any!

> *Journal – July 7th, 1983*
>
> *How many hours lost in the adventurous pursuit of illicit sex? Either passively or actively, the days are filled with "minute" undertakings that slowly add up into the hundreds if not thousands over the years.*

Friday: I had more meetings to try and sell advertising and managed to sell one ad space. Did shopping at night. I also called Victor who suggested going to the gay bar but I had to take a pass. It's too tricky to pull off in this tiny community, even now with what I've got with Coo. He does seem genuine though . . . We'll have to wait and see. I dropped in on Da. Ml. Chatted for quite a while. Went to the ABS and had an encounter with one of the regulars.

> *Journal – July 8th, 1983*
>
> *I'm back into a slew of activity and unfortunately old habits are all that's being serviced.*
>
> *I'm feeling the pressures imposed on my own body. The intensity is remarkable in that it lasts, has lasted for so long. There is no cure, only a slow death now.*
>
> *In vain, I don't try to conquer it anymore, I simply succumb. It's a bottomless pit from which escape is unheard of as far as I'm aware.*

Saturday: Is my time here being wasted? I certainly hope not. Trying to type up what there is of *From Now On*. Took a nap late in the afternoon and went swimming at night. The cute blond lifeguard came in while I was showering. Now, why did I sense as though the timing was intentional on his part . . . ?

Sunday: Finished typing up all that I've written so far of *From Now On*, and I added the last of the confrontation scenes between Tim and James. Last night's heavy conversation with Coo was so evocative of my past with Monsieur. Poor Coo, this is the only way I know how to do this breakup. A purple blotch on my lower backside sent my entire being into a sate of fear and paranoia. Is AIDS to be my demise? At night we saw *Night of the Shooting Stars*.

The Week of July 11th – 17th

Monday: Ran around doing errands for co-op ads. It started to rain so heavily around noon, I felt imprisoned in my own home. My money came through for the desk commercial. What a farce. The pool wasn't opened to the public at night so I couldn't swim. Met Mk. Pa. for a bite to eat. The ABS was crowded when I went there today. I found myself having this tedious incident with one of the regulars. I just didn't want to have a go with him but he was *so* persistent. I had no choice but to leave the place.

Journal – July 11th, 1983

Last night's late bedtime discussion reminded me of all the painful talks Monsieur and I had back in the day. Though now it was my turn to speak Monsieur's words. I know now how it felt to be him and I could empathize with Coo so terribly.

She left and went outside till dawn and I wasn't able to fall asleep until her return. And today I find deadly purple patches on my backside. Early warning signs of AIDS, or is it simply a bruise? Should I seek some kind of medical advice . . . ? I'll have to keep a close watch and see what develops.

Tuesday: My boredom just builds up, doesn't it? I write, I type, I masturbate. I write, I eat, I swim, I go to the ABS, I masturbate, I write alone seeking the solitude it brings but strangely never finding it; seeking love/sex for all the wrong reasons. I run amuck. What will the morrows bring?

Wednesday: Forget about the tomorrows—I ended up doing Valium and drinking, then calling Se. up only to find out he's been gambling away all of his money. Something about the news so disturbed me . . . I left a note for Coo, who had gone out with Mk. Pa., saying I was going out for the night. I slept over at Da. Ml.'s. He made sense about no more fucking around, but can I do it? It was so beautiful being in his bed again. No sex but some early morning cuddling grounded me. Went for a swim, read, wrote and saw National Theatre production of *Treats* tonight. Excellent piece.

Thursday: The days are frustratingly alike. My dedication to my writing is on a par with my need for sexual gratification/titillation. Whether swimming, riding or walking, my eyes roam for the possibility of encounters. I discovered a new WC watering hole. Oy gevalt! Coo went out to a party with Mk. Pa. and I got stoned and went to bed early enough. Had a long talk with Da. Ml. again. Coo and I put our deposit down for the truck for our move to LA.

Friday: Slept in, hung over badly from so little booze. Kind of depressing. Swam twice and did some more typing of edits. Got monies from ad sales. I'm thinking of going out to LA with Da. Ml. next weekend to buy a car and find us an apartment but I'm not sure that it's a wise choice.

Journal – July 15th, 1983

The scent of death is compulsion.

Saturday: Ron brought over some flagstone and then Coo and I went outside of town to get more up in the hills. We're still short of our goal. I went swimming. Same routine. No mail.

Sunday: Nothing changes much. We bought clothes for Coo today. Hopefully it's the last of our splurges out here. Da. Ml. said it was okay to drive out with him if he does go to LA next weekend. Here it is that we'll soon be off into the wild blue yonder once again. Saw *The Flight of the Eagle*. Added more plot to my storyline for *Cooperative Murder*.

The Week of
July 18ᵗʰ – 24ᵗʰ

Monday: Getting ready to leave. The plans become more and more set. The next two weeks are recorded in my journal.

Tuesday: (no entry)

Wednesday: (no entry)

Thursday: (see journal)

Journal – July 21ˢᵗ, 1983

Is this another familiar date? Someone's birthday from my past? An occasion of some importance from my past? Why does it stand out like this . . .

My body has goose bumps as I write, a sense that poetry is rising to the surface, boiling over to be jotted down as first impressions.

I finished typing up the latest edit/revision of Co-operative Murder. *I continue to vacillate about the quality of the writing. Why am I so ambivalent, almost complacent about this upcoming voyage? Am I not ready for the direction I'm headed in? Hollywood? Who* does *go there, and for what? Is there even something waiting there for me to find? I hope. I've said this so often before, but I'm ready for whatever comes down the pike.*

Driving with Da. Ml. was trippy. He's so darn cute. He taught me the basics on how to drive a stick shift. After a few tentative starts I got under way. We arrived in Phoenix in one piece and not overly tired. Met Ro. L., very good-looking and quite pleasant. I was a little antsy at first, worried that I'd be corralled into some kind of threesome that I couldn't handle but everything relaxed after a swim and supper.

Afterwards, I took off on my own with the car hoping to explore the town. Went to one ABS and they actually kicked me out. What gives with that?! This guy there wanted to know if I felt like partying with him and his girlfriend but it sounded too risky so I decided against it. I left there and after the car stalled on me a number of times I proceeded to find the next ABS. Of course the cops would stop me on my way there. I had no idea of the address where I was staying, nor could I recall Ro. L.'s last name or his phone number. I also didn't know where W. or D., whose car I was driving, lived back in LA. I was so nervous at first, I said the car belonged to Ji. Se. back in Santa Fe.

I felt foolish, though I could see the humor in my situation. I didn't even match the picture on my license because of the new hair color, and I was having <u>such</u> a difficult time driving the stick shift that the officer even told me not to move until they had driven off! When I got inside the second ABS, my first trick shoved his finger up my ass just seconds after going down on me.

I practically shit myself from the shock and the pain. I know that my scream could be heard across the entire store. But the second guy I hooked up with was a perfect fantasy. He was this drunken straight guy who let me do what I wanted to him—except that he spoke just a tad too loudly and didn't want me to come. He kept asking me to go somewhere with him, which of course I didn't want—I just wanted to come, but I played it out his way for a while before coming and then left. It was certainly nice, if strange.

And yes, more cops came around the corner just as I was trying to get back to Ro. L.'s place, but no one stopped me this time out. When I got back to the house I shared my cop story with them. Had a late night swim. If Ro. L. and I had been alone I might have been tempted to make a pass, but knowing what he's into would just have been wasting both of our time. And so . . . here I sit jotting down these few lines. LA here I come. If there is good karma coming my way, it would be very nice if it came within this next week. Please!

Friday: (no entry)

Saturday: (see journal)

Journal – July 23rd, 1983

Got into LA early last night and went to look at cars. I finally decided on this cute '77 Toyota Celica GT. Left there to attend this lesbian fête—met some in-

teresting people. Today, I went to do this audition and Co. Ma. turned out to be the assistant producer and St. Ma. (from NYC) was there as well to audition. It was nice to see both of them. Of what I read, the part seemed written for me. I mean, eerily so, but the quality of the talent on the project, at least from what I could see today, left much to be desired.

Then I went over to meet Je. Gates. My heart skipped a few beats. He reminded me of Monsieur and looked like a younger Jo. Mi. Of course he's straight, which is why I had to hold back. He had the most beautiful eyes and the sweetest demeanor! It was a tad awkward towards the end—having touched on so many topics. And yes, I'd prattled on at the mouth as usual.

I came home to find zero parking near Nl.'s apartment building. I did look at a few places on my way back there but nothing worthwhile. Went out to ABS later on and met this guy, Jim. We went to this secluded alley and had a lovely time under a full moon. Then I took off for Studio One. Everything was the same, no one asks anyone to dance and if they do ask, they're usually refused. What strange, sad attitudes.

Sunday: (see journal)

Journal – July 24th, 1983

Sunday afternoon and feeling very hungover. All this drinking and smoking isn't helping matters at all. Did some shopping. A friend of Nl.'s came over while he was out. Actually Nl. is still out and will be for the rest of the day. We managed to talk last night. He resents what I'm doing to Coo. I can't blame him, as Coo's long-time friend I can understand where he's coming from—though he doesn't really know me from a hole in the ground. Started to look at more places. It was too late for this one studio apartment on this street. It would have been a dream come true. The gay guys around the pool here are so trippy. You just can't join the group it seems . . .

Journal – July 24th, 1983

Late Sunday night and I'm in turmoil, a familiar place but <u>so</u> unexpected. I feel stunned and rather hopeless.

I came home to find the few dishes that I had left in the sink—four to be exact—had been cleaned. That was my first premonition, though why, I'm not sure. My bedding was out and there were no notes as in previous nights, etc. It was only halfpast twelve so the hour wasn't <u>that</u> late. I casually opened Nl.'s bedroom door to see if he might still be awake and he flew into a startled rage that lasted a good thirty seconds. I told him I was sorry and closed the door ASAP.

So now my mind is racing with a million scenarios about what might be awaiting me in the morning.

The Week of
July 25th – 31st

Monday: (see journal)

Journal – July 25th, 1983

A tense depression is settling in and I'm trying to fight against it. I had my first car accident today. I was rear-ended from the side. I hope the guy takes his responsibility seriously and pays me my deductible or else I'm fucked. I have zero experience that could have prepared me for this one. I surprised myself at how calm I was in getting all the necessary information. Thanks to too much TV viewing! Still, I find it hard to believe that this can be resolved so easily. I settled the home front situation in part, though a feeling of miscommunication still exists between Nl. and me. The talent agency visit seemed a total waste of my time. Of course, now I'm thinking of doing <u>aliya</u>! Is Israel ready? Am I?!

Tuesday: (see journal)

Journal – July 26th, 1983

A long day. Got a quick estimate at Hollywood Toyota, then drove to downtown LA to drop off insurance stuff and over to the passport office. I had to wait an hour to get my photo, and then ran around to get the notary public to sign off. Left and went out to Santa Monica. It wasn't as great as I'd hoped and there were no vacancies that I could locate, certainly none within my budget. I came home to try and set up times for some appointments. I can't really get a photo shoot set up until I'm back in Santa Fe. I guess that's okay. I get prints tomorrow if all goes well.

I found a few nice places but none that I liked enough to sign a lease. Then I met Nl.'s friend, Mv., and we hit it off quite well. He managed to seduce me, sort of, and of course I succumbed. What else is new! It's not that I feel used exactly, but . . . I wonder what he'll think of my writing.

Wednesday: (see journal)

Journal – July 27th, 1983

Da. Ml. finally called me first thing in the morning and asked me over to meet the two Ga.s. Well I don't know how Ga. Do. felt, but I heard bells ringing. There was such a buzz from the chemistry between us; all one-sided I'm sure, but damn it was strong. The other Ga.

seemed very nice, though they struck me as an odd duo. Then again, maybe that's why they've been together so long?

When Ga. Do. put me on that machine and started to play with my lower back, I actually thought I was going to come in my jeans. Between his laid-back attitude and his looks, I was a goner. He reminded me so much of that actor from the commune on Lowther up in Toronto, the guy who did Elephant Man *on Broadway. And ironically, the two G.'s had just met that actor here in LA.*

Even though the guy said I was cute—and he felt that he just <u>had</u> to cuddle me, or some such thing—I seriously doubt he was feeling any of what I was feeling.

Da. Ml. and I had a quick and too expensive bite to eat so that by the time I got back to Nl.'s apartment I'd missed Patrick dropping off the photos for me. I took off a bit later to meet up with the man who rear–ended me and he gave me the cash we'd agreed on. I looked around at some more apartments but they're either too expensive or real dumps.

Bought some wine and left to go to dinner at St. Ma. Had a pleasant time with good food and good conversation. He even showed me a picture I gave him of me with a few lines of poetry I'd written for him on the back of it. I'd forgotten all about that. He had tickets for the Hollywood Bowl and afterwards we came back to his place for a bit. He's as nice as when we hooked up in NYC and he's certainly interesting but he drinks a lot more than I remembered. I wonder if perhaps he's someone who gets really angry when love relationships get tricky. Still, is this one worth rekindling? I can't say . . .

Thursday: (see journal)

Journal – July 28th, 1983

I'm trying to deal with the casting of the part that I wanted in Mixed Blessings. *That I accidentally happened to find out how much the actor is getting for the gig, doesn't make it any better. What can you do! Israel here we come?!*

Journal – July 28th, later on . . .

This world is so wearisome at times. I'm trying to deal with Nl. The kindest person can also be the biggest neurotic. I know it's the pot calling the kettle black here. How ironic that all of my neuroses are being met with more of the same by him! Even though he can't control my life in the slightest he does try his best, leaving me in the lurch in the middle of discussions, and me wondering if it's "all in my head" or if he's seriously going deaf.

Why he feels a need to answer questions with only more questions or glib one-liners is a fascinating study, but I don't have time for this drama now. His perceptions of me are <u>so</u> negative. I confess that I can be stupid, that I have paranoid tendencies and my energy is "up there," but I'm not all these things at once and certainly not all *of them all of the time. This attitude of his is driving me crazy.*

Thank goodness this visit is soon coming to an end. I'll give tomorrow my best shot in collecting more information and dealing with car problems. But I feel like not much else can be done in LA for now. Coo will have to find the apartment that she wants and I will have to decide what's best for me at some later date. If Israel can do it for me, then that's what I'll be doing.

Luck will be the deciding factor in all of this.

Friday: (no entry)

Saturday: (no entry)

Sunday: Got back into Santa Fe around 10 AM and called up Coo for her to come and pick me up. No sooner in then Ge. called to inform me that he was back in town all week. Umm . . . Slept away the day. Talked over things with Coo. Started editing *Cooperative Murder*.

Journal – July 31st, 1983

I'm back in Santa Fe after a 26-hour ordeal on Trailway Buses. The cast of characters was mind-boggling. Too tired though to describe them for now.

I slept a lot of the day away. No sooner down for an afternoon nap than Ge.'s message arrived. He was back in town for the week. Oy gevalt. I wonder if Victor will be as keen to hear from me. I doubt it somehow.

> *There was some tension at the house but otherwise okay. The flowers and the gardens are blooming as though jungle fever had set in. I spoke briefly with Da. Ml. and with Mk. Pa. Now for a month of serious writing.*

The Week of
August 1ˢᵗ – 7ᵗʰ

Monday: Got a card from Monsieur informing me that he wasn't coming out. Figures! Corrected and wrote new piece for newspaper. Made some calls, trying to figure things out. At night, around suppertime, Da. Ml. called in his role as one of the producers and criticized Coo on her bio that she'd submitted for the *Mixed Blessings* program. Such hoopla over nothing. In the end, I'm the one that suffers over the whole mess. M. Engler, D. Farber's ex, ignored me when he saw me today, and Mk. Pa. confessed to me his affair with Coo while I was out of town. Good for her!

Tuesday: The setting here is like a small bittersweet movie. Coo leaves on Thursday to rehearse in LA and nothing will ever be quite the same again for us, for our life together. Hopefully only good will come of it. Worked a modeling class in the morning and brought in some photos for the newspaper article. Got stoned.

Wednesday: Did another modeling class and some writing. Went swimming and then over to the ABS. Had a boring time. Got stoned again. A last farewell for Coo. It's sad to have it come to an end like this. It was so unemotional, though, that it left me confused. Monsieur called tonight. We had an okay conversation.

Journal – Aug. 3rd, 1983

Spoke with Monsieur. It was nice to hear his voice.

I am in such limbo. The night before Coo's departure for Los Angeles to start rehearsals for Mixed Blessings *and to begin her relocation plans. I'll have over two weeks to do as I please but I need to concentrate every ounce of energy on my writing.*

Thursday: Coo left early this morning and Ge. called almost as soon as I had returned from the shuttle drop off. Wrote and napped and then did my last modeling session for Albert Handel's seminar. Ge. came over later on. It was boring because he's so detached from the sex that it becomes almost totally one-sided, it seems. I stayed up for a while longer after he left.

Journal – Aug. 4th, 1983

Well, Ge. came over—is that all there is . . . ? Not to be too cruel since he's probably quite typical of his cohort in America today. There's no self-knowledge at all that I can decipher. As for my temporary bachelorhood,

> *it's just dawning on me but with surprisingly little enticement—just some peace and solitude to look forward to.*

Friday: Up early to go down to Albuquerque for a photo session and my usual pit stop at the ABS. More like AIDS 101! I came back to Santa Fe and saw the *Pericles* production by Mk. Pa.'s BAI class. It was so-so. I found myself attracted to this guy in the audience who turned out to be Mk. Pa.'s latest paramour, Dn. But of course! Stayed in at night, sleeping on and off. Se. called from Toronto, then Stu. Ma. called me from Los Angeles. That spurred me to telephone Coo.

Journal – Aug. 5th, 1983

How will these words sit with me in the years to come? How redundant will the repetition be?

This house will always remain quaint, at least the memory of it. I'll think of these times and will recall where each and every bric-a-brac was placed in these adobe rooms. How perfect the picture seemed; how bittersweet that the end to our marriage came here in the land of supposed enchantment.

All the landscaping work we did in the yard is like a small monument that we leave behind, a memento of who we were.

In my crazy, uncontrolled world of lust, the game narrows with each case of AIDS reported. If not now, when?

Saturday: Another day of personal solitude. I do love the challenge of this solo flight, unafraid, yet feeling totally psychotic about it all! I went swimming at night and then off to Zorro's. A few people from R. & J. production were there, as was Tom Gartner. I had an interesting time if just a bit too drunk to fully appreciate it. I did speak with Gartner but I doubt if I left any great impression. He told me that M. Engler may be his assistant next year. *Ah la vie, la vie*! Ended up bringing Jim home. It was nice but typical.

Sunday: A day lost to sleep and recovery. Did a little bit of writing. Spoke to Mk. Pa and went dancing with him briefly later on but I had a boring, negative time. Swam in the late afternoon and dropped by Cine X place. Got felt up by some dirty old man and did much the same to someone else. We consummated the act back in my car. God, but this is so boring.

Journal – Aug. 7th, 1983

All these years into these bodily pursuits—the whole experience leaves me feeling blank, <u>as if</u> I didn't know the outcome or the rules!

Journal – Aug. 7th, later on . . .

If I could only sustain some of the inspiration that takes over me when I'm in gay bars and seedy porno establishments. Nothing is to be found there except the repetition of cheap tricks unless I use it all as fodder for my fiction. What can I do to break those habits?

Alone, I'm at leisure to choose and I do so, freely and irresponsibly. They're my messes for me to endure.

> *I invited M. Engler over for coffee today but he declined. I wonder if he'll look me up or just ignore that we're neighbors for a few weeks. Hard one to predict.*

The Week of
August 8th – 14th

Monday: I'm as productive as I need to be, I guess. I did some writing and spoke to Coo twice. Also called John Scagliotti back in NYC and made a call to Social Services in Los Angeles to research some facts for some material in *From Now On*. Went to swim twice, read a little, drank some wine and took a few naps; a wonderfully luxurious day if you think about it. M. Engler did drop by and we chatted amicably enough, considering the disparity in our outlooks on Direct Centering. From what I could see, he still adheres to their tenets. At night, I met Mk. Pa. for a bite and we took a walk around the Plaza.

> *Journal – Aug. 8th, 1983*
>
> *M. Engler just dropped by. I was happy to see that he chose to come over after all. As I expected, our conversation focused on Direct Centering and D. Farber, with the usual deadlocked arguments that follows either topic. Still, we both managed to hold our ground and work through it.*

So how did I feel about his visit . . . ? I felt a bit put on the spot at first, disturbed not so much by his cool exterior but by the almost total lack of emotional life coming from him. Who can say what will come of his affiliation with that movement in the long run, but what I saw today was scary. Whether I'll ever be working with him at some time in the future is doubtful, but you never know.

On my end, putting my career in perspective, I can see that there's been irreparable damage done by this long decade of trying to get somewhere with my acting career. I'm sure that my regional credits from back in Canada have some measure of worth but this long decade of waiting, hoping for a big break, has taken its toll.

Tuesday: An interesting day. Had dinner with Lee Lw., a lovely time. Two of her friends dropped by and we all got stoned together. I left to go home and then went out dancing with Mk. Pa. Did some driving around, cruising about town afterwards, but no action.

Wednesday: Woke up with an awful sore throat so I slept on and off all day. Did Coo call? I can't remember. Went to see *La Nuit de Varennes*. Loved some of it. Marcello Mastroianni was superb as Casanova. I did manage to write a lot today.

Thursday: It's all the same repetition. Slept away the day. Co. Mi. called from NYC and we chatted for quite a while. Saw *Risky Business*. Very entertaining. Had coffee with Mk. Pa. Did a good amount of writing. A. Buresch called out of the blue. Of course, she's in need of cash! Will try to help out. Went out to Zorro's later on and ended up the night with Ge. Talked with D. Bell who said he could read success in my face. Ah, if only the Fates could hear and pay attention to <u>him</u>, right?!

> *Journal – Aug. 11th, 1983*
>
> *Same old thing—cigarettes and beer and gay bars. Never changes, never will. I was quoted tonight as saying, "Reality is fine, just as long as it's done well." I concur!*

Friday: Gosh, every night I return to Zorro's. It's impossible to tell one night from the other. After a long and, at times, heavy phone conversation with Coo I got stoned and went back there. Co-op worker St. was there with a deaf friend. Poor St., to lose a lover, be raped and then get fired, all in quick succession like that! Completed *Zyz. Queendoms* first draft.

Saturday: Started typing up *Z.Q.* Brought in bike at the Honda dealership. Let's hope they can sell it for me before we leave for LA. I got a ride back into town with the father of one of the kids in *R. & J.* Bopped around downtown and bought a card for Coo. Bumped into Bb. Went dancing at night with lots of cuties out to troll. This stunner I asked to dance turned out to be *so* out of it! I managed to place a few more faces from the ABS in Albuquerque.

Journal – Aug. 13th, 1983

How to write down the redundancy you find in bars! The sad reality is that most people never really find anyone there, just fleeting looks in pairs of attractive eyes. All those faces coming at you, so similar in their lack of expectation. At least I find dance partners, for the most part.

The first man tonight to stir anything within me could hardly stand up. Things just went from bad to worse from there. There was the nice hairdresser, then it was Juan, Ji.'s friend, but because Ji. was there that was out of the question. Then it was a Jean, followed by a Jeremiah, and finally Bi. from the co-op. I wouldn't have minded bedding him but he was with a friend so that also wasn't in the cards. Like the song says, "It's Raining Men," but I'm not sure about the hallelujah part.

I called Se. last night and when he asked if there was anything wrong, the only answer I had for him was "life." Nothing too complicated there, just life!

Had a long talk with Coo that left me so sad in so many ways. So what did I do? I got stoned and went out dancing. What else!

Journal – Aug. 13th, cont'd . . .

I go to the liquor cabinet with such decisiveness, as though I would be cheating myself if I denied myself a nice tall drink.

Sunday: Slept in late. Typed for a bit then took a nice long walk around downtown. Mailed off my card to Coo. Mk. Pa. came over to watch a movie on HBO and I finished typing up *Z.Q.* Pornography is so deceptive. It's all so real until you've come. Then you' re just left with a picture in mind and some sticky fingers . . .

The Week of
August 15th – 21st

Monday: IRS gave us a bit of unhappy news with their bill so I had to deal with that bullshit. At night, Ge. came over and we had a great time together. I even cut his hair. As I enter these pages, it's already Thursday and he's off to Hawaii, to further his education and on to his new life. Good luck, Ge. Stayed up late with Mk. Pa. *Je suis rempli de vie et en même temps je meure.*

> *Journal – Aug. 15th, 1983*
>
> *Last time with Ge., I think . . . Of course it <u>would</u> have to be a great time, this time around. He seemed more responsive, started to let loose and be more relaxed. Now, <u>that</u> fantasy is off to his Hawaiian paradise. We showered together and then he got me to trim his hair. The full treatment here! Still, I don't want to underestimate any of it. It's been a learning curve, what with our age difference. Hard to believe this has even taken place. I wonder what kind of growth potential he has ahead of*

him. Well goodnight for now. If we meet tomorrow I'm sure it can't but be anticlimactic, but perhaps it will be nicer than I care to admit.

Tuesday: Did a few errands and some writing. Sent off money to A. Buresch in Paris. I wonder if I'll ever see that money again. At night, I ended up wasting my time and my cash at Cine X. Oy! Spoke with Coo. She hasn't found us an LA apartment as yet and her new car broke down. Shit, there goes more money.

Wednesday: Got up early to get some things accomplished. Got copies made of *Z. Q.* Met this illustrator, P. Co., at the copy place. I saw her work and liked it enough that I took a chance and gave her a copy of *Z. Q.* to look at. Time ticks on. Saw *Billy Bishop Goes to War*. I'd love to tackle that vehicle for myself at some later date. Spoke to Coo.

Thursday: I went out to dance with Mk. Pa. Had a nice enough time but people's attitudes with all the affectation is just too much—all these ditsy ladies with these stunning boys leaving trails of beauty on the dance floor. Read excerpts from my *In Search of Gold* collection and decided to type it all up. Stayed at it till 4 AM—not that I'd care for that material to see the light of day during my lifetime, that's for sure.

Friday: Finished part III of *From Now On*. Harvested our sole surviving pot plant, a pity that it never flowered. Went for my daily walk. At night I saw these short Buddhist films at the Folk Art Museum. Ke. Ki. was there. It was a very spiritual evening. After our extended talk,

I now feel a need to investigate the possibility of St. John's College. I spoke with Coo and called up Se. in Toronto.

> *Journal – Aug. 19th, 1983*
>
> *Just got back from seeing Parts I and II of this Buddhist trilogy, The Field of the Senses; such powerful material. It left me in awe of what I know exists out there.*
>
> *The sight of a burning corpse going off into the continuation of light along with the words spoken left little to the imagination. The spiritual uplift was enhanced by meeting Ke. Ki., the guy who played B. in R. & J. Such a gentle person.*
>
> *That he attended St. John's and that he wants to do graduate work at U. of T. added to my fascination with him. Of course I can't deny the lust factor, too, but his appeal had as much to do with his mind as his physique. And yes, all together now, he's totally straight. His suggestion that I look into the undergraduate program at St. John's gave me food for thought.*
>
> *The Annapolis campus he talked about sounds more to my liking. Once again a fantasy takes root?*
>
> *I finished part III of* From Now On.

Saturday: Woke up early and got to work typing. I took a nap before going down to Indian Market on the Plaza. There were too many people crowding the artwork and I found too much similarity in the products that were for sale. I left and cruised around for a while. Went swimming and then home to type some more. Got stoned and went out to Zorro's. Jim was there. Even though I could have probably ended the night with him, I went after this older guy who turned out to be a Frenchman, in from Texas. We didn't go to bed together.

Journal – Aug. 20th, 1983

Back at the ABS, just one night after such great promises to resist . . . The story goes something like this: A beautiful enough of a guy, reminded me of someone, may even have met him there before. We spent I don't know how many quarters just checking each other out. Finally we decided to go into the same booth, but as soon as we were inside he quickly set up rules: absolutely <u>no</u> touching. I even tried a few times but he was adamant in saying "no!" All he wanted to do was to watch me come. So of course, at that point, I couldn't even get it up. Finally, barely half-erect, he manages to come and in a touching moment, he presses the bareness of his leg onto mine as I come like a firecracker going off.

The dialogue that ensued, something about a Kleenex and then him saying, "You must think I'm fucking weird." All I could reply was, "No. But you should stay away from those poppers." Then I left.

I should have said that in this post-AIDS/herpes era, you probably did us both a favor. As I came home it dawned on me. Did he indeed have either of those diseases?

Sunday: Coo arrived home from her LA rehearsals. It's nice to see her again. She went out for supper with the cast and I went to see *Mr. Mom*. I realized today how it irks me, the way Coo speaks to Mk. Pa. over the phone. Redid our tax materials for 1982.

The Week of
August 22nd – 28th

Monday: Coo was at rehearsals all day. Went to do errands and got a few more things for our dinner tomorrow for the cast. Had a quickie in the library loo.

Tuesday: Shopped and prepped food for our dinner party. Met Dick Sergeant. People seemed to enjoy themselves. The meal was over before I knew it. I found myself a bit intimidated by the director. Hard to believe he was C. Crawford's husband. I went to see their dress rehearsal at night. It was okay. Coo was fine, as I knew she would be. We got stoned when she got back. Coo made a small gay dig and I felt the need to confront her on it. It stopped there.

Wednesday: Brought back the IBM Selectric. It feels like I've just lost my lifeline yet again. I opted to get my left ear pierced and I now have two studs in place. At night, saw *Long Good Friday Weekend*. Liked it. At the ABS I saw this guy I hadn't seen since the winter, this beautiful man, by the name of John.

> *Journal – Aug. 24th, 1983*
>
> *Coo just left for the theatre for the first preview of* Mixed Blessings. *It's been ages for her. I just know she'll be great. She's such a trouper!*
>
> *Her period is two days late. Let's hope she hasn't been "foolish" in her personal affairs. Though drama and melodrama has led us to this present existence we're calling life, I'd hate for her to have to make a decision on an abortion at this particular juncture.*
>
> *Since this could be a last chance for her at motherhood, who knows what choice she might make were she faced with that. Let's hope we're not in for episode #10 of Coo's folly!*

Thursday: Another opening, another show. It went well according to all. I only showed up after the show as planned. Nl., Coo's mom and D. Farber all called during the day. Went to this lovely place up on Tano Road for their opening night party. It was strange to see all of Jayce's Texan buddies at the event, good-looking and all *very* straight, down to the very last one. I managed to back us into a ditch at the end of the evening and ended up sitting in our car with Coo, Jo. H., Linda and Phoebe, playing word games while waiting for AAA to show up to tow us out.

Friday: Slept in and then started to pack up the house for our big move to LA. We went to Linda's party at night. We didn't stay too late but again, all this drinking, this smoking we're doing, it just takes a toll. Jo. H. asked if we could all get together once before we left town. Coo and I got stoned back at the house and stayed up watching some TV. Did a lot of talking about the status of our relationship.

Saturday: Spent most of the day packing. At night, I tried to call Jo. H. but couldn't find his number anywhere. Sent cards to Ann B. and D. Farber. After the show, when Coo got home, we got stoned and made love. How sane was that? It's like being on a cancer ward and getting a boost from an old tried and true drug.

Sunday: This was a matinee day for Coo. I spent some time talking with Jo. H. I guess I was wrong about him; doesn't take away the fact that I'd bed him in a heartbeat. The party at the Seldon's was lovely. Had a good swim, great wine and food. There was table service. How's that for posh! Mat. T. really opened up, chatting up everyone. Now is the time for all good boys to go to sleep. The week ahead is going to be a killer!

The Week of
August 29th – September 4th

Monday: I ran errands in the morning and then we took off to Albuquerque and the mountains in the afternoon. Being up there again was exquisite. Before we left I went to St. John's to set up my permission from the Dean to attend their first seminar of the year on *The Iliad*. It was a bit more of a hassle than I'd expected at first but the situation was finally resolved in my favor. At night we went to Club West for reggae. It was just so-so. The rest of the cast never even showed up.

Tuesday: The days are spent packing and planning and vice versa. The show at night went very well. Afterwards, Coo and I went with Rick and Patty to the Soak.

Wednesday: Ah, mysterious 24 hours of possibilities. I spent the afternoon and evening with Jo. H. Leaving him at night, with a kiss, was as romantic as one could hope for. My meeting with the dean at St. John's was short and basically felt unnecessary from my end. Still, I'm reading Homer's *Iliad*. Reading, reading, reading.

Thursday: The day spent getting ready for the seminar, trying to read as much of *The Iliad* as I could. Eighteen of those chapters leave one's mind boggled but rejuvenated. The poetry soars within my veins and I do feel quite alive from it all. The seminar was all I could have asked for *and* more. It convinced me of where I need to be this time next year! Now for the planning of that desire. The party at Betty Garrett's was fine.

Friday: We went for lunch at Na. & El. Ma.'s. Lovely food and good conversation. Hate to say goodbye to them. Came home to more packing. At night, I believe I went to see Jo. H., but I'm not sure as I write these entries in retrospect. Probably though. We went and got a bottle of wine and sipped and talked. Love, as it overtakes you, is such an exquisite thing.

Journal – Sept. 2nd, 1983

Massive dose of depression sets in. Reasons, too numerous to figure out.

At the bank this morning, this guy was there who was in last night's seminar up at the College. I would have liked to introduce myself but I was with Coo and I couldn't figure out how to manage that. Of course it only set off a longing for what I have and don't have.

The fact is that I certainly want to get into St. John's in Annapolis for next fall. That, in turn, means I need money, which means work, work, work.

"How to attend college in ten difficult steps" might very well define my time in Los Angeles. Which raises the question: why bother being there if I'm not going to take advantage of the acting career opportunities it has to offer? Can I do that while pursuing putting money aside to go to college? That's if I can even get accepted there!

And now there's this Jo. H., that lovely name, that lovely face. What am I going to do with that? Very little. I leave so soon. Both of us are attached and there seems to be no reason to tackle the tribulations of a lovemaking session. Is that what it means to grow up?!

Saturday: The shit hit the fan as we dealt with a major fuckup at the truck rental place. We ended up having to settle for a 24-footer truck from U-Haul instead of our original rental company. Da. Ml. will now be driving our Santa Fe car out to LA next week since we couldn't tow our car on the back of this large size of a truck. We packed most of the remainder of our things today with Mk. Pa.'s help. Then it was off to a lovely luncheon at the Egoff's. I lucked out at having Betty Garrett at my table so there wasn't a dull second to be had. Later in the afternoon, I penned a poem for Jo. H. Tentative title is "Love's Ally." I gave it to him at night. We said goodbye after going with the cast to Vanessie's for a drink. It was certainly confusing. So much possibility but not the right time?

Sunday: I got up early to finish packing. Coo did her last show. I watched all of it. We said goodbye to everyone, to our landlord, Mk. Pa., Da. Ml., then had a hell of a time to get that fucking massive truck out of the circular drive inside our compound. It turned out that we had a faulty left light and our high beams kept going on and off as well as the yellow lights. Add to that Berkely's *constant* mewing and we ended up smoking like fiends till we reached Gallup and crashed for the night inside the cab.

The Week of
September 5th – 11th

Monday: Can it be Monday and Labor Day already? We left early to hit the road. Coo finally agreed to drive the monster truck in the morning. We managed to run out of gas just outside of Flagstaff. This great police officer helped us as well as this trucker who stopped his rig at the top of a hill and came back down on foot to back our truck further off the highway and onto the gravel. According to him we were sitting ducks to be hit from behind. Other than that, we've been managing okay! It's hard to believe that Santa Fe is behind us.

Tuesday: We came into LA around 5:30 AM after a grueling day of mishaps. The last of which was an accident in Needles, CA, where we "borrowed" part of the overhang at the drive-thru at a McDonald's. God, what an experience! The driving was *so* intense coming down the grapevine as we tried to control our speed and not veer into other lanes. Once in LA, we walked around until it was time to go over to Wor. for our keys, etc. There was no answer at first but after a bit of a hassle, we got into the apartment. At night, Mv. drove us to Ki. & Ar.'s to pick up our other car that Coo had left with them.

Wednesday: A long day. We were up around 7:30 to unpack most of our belongings that were still left in the truck. Nl. showed up very late, and Andy P. dropped by, too. It was nice to see a friendly face. We left to meet Sol Ac., our new accountant. He was great. He's married to the original Dolly Dimples from the *Our Gang* series. Drove home along boy's town and bought some paint and a shower curtain. We spent the evening playing interior decorators. Called Pt. Wh. who told me she's trying to put together a film version of *Splendora* and would love me for the lead! We'll see about that.

Thursday: We returned the truck and got a bit further with our unpacking. Painted the remainder of the bookshelves. Saw *Zelig*, not that great. The place is starting to look habitable for humans.

Friday: This was phone day. We spent all day waiting for the damn thing to get installed and for the caretaker to install new locks on door and mailbox. The weather is very hot—unbearably hot—humid and muggy. Coo went to drop off some pictures and resume and I had an interview for this French play that turned out to be a waste of my time. They were *so* snobbish. Our place is almost all set up. Got stoned and crashed.

Saturday: Slept in. Wrote letters to home, to Jo. H. and A. H., and cards to Ann B. and Co. Mi. We drove out to Santa Monica to check out their food co-op. Coo made plans to go out to Mat. T.'s place for tomorrow. How long will Coo and me last together in this environment I wonder?

Sunday: Wrote more letters in the morning and then we went out to Mat. T.'s in the Valley. Had a great time by the pool. Met Wor. and his wife, Ma. El. There was also a casting director and this stage director, Jon—an interesting mix of people overall. We came home to a noisy back alleyway and to rude, inconsiderate neighbor tenants. Welcome back to the real world, T.!

The Week of
September 12th – 18th

Monday: Can't recall the day too much. Did phone calling, banking, and food shopping. At night got stoned and watched *Twelve Angry Men*.

Tuesday: Filed for unemployment, which was pretty quick and easy out here. I hope this time it comes through without too many complications. Coo went out for an audition while I stayed home writing. At night, I went over to Mv.'s. Great conversation. He took a few shots of me, ostensibly to finish his roll of film. God, I hope he returns them to me, puhlease!

Wednesday: Did an interview for a part in *Travesties*. It was okay but I doubt if anything comes of it. Went to

SAG and then to this gay bookstore, Different Light. The guys that run it are Canadians, and two of them knew John Lindfield! At night, Coo and I went for ice cream in boys' town and then for a stroll along Melrose after getting stoned with Cathy. Decided to go dancing at Florentine Gardens. The place is huge.

Thursday: Leisurely day reading *Splendora*. The more I read the novel the more I want to do the project. My pictures came in today and they were spotted. There's no charge, but I still have no pictures to get going around here. Decided to order some postcards as well. We went out for supper with Wo. and Ma. El., and then home for wine and cookies. Had this heated conversation over one topic after another.

Friday: Went out and bought a new phone. Got back just in time as Da. Ml. arrived with our other car. We dropped him off at his friend's place. At night, Dick Sergeant gave us comp tickets to see *Chaplin*. Had great seats for a so-so musical. Loved the theatre complex where it was playing.

Saturday: Wrote letters, mostly killing time till we went out at night to see *Caligula* with Mat. T. and his wife, Gl. Had a pleasant night but got too stoned and drank way too much.

Sunday: Slept in. Went out to Pasadena to audition for a waiver theatre gig. I'm not right for the part. I was peeved at the omission in the trades on the height requirement for the role. Still, the audition went well. Came back to town and went over with Coo to finally meet her friend Sn., along with about seven other gay boys. Had fun, but somehow it felt awkward. Spoke to Stu. Ma. at night. Do I stand a chance to get into his show?

The Week of
September 19th – 25th

Monday: Auditioned for the national company of *Brighton Beach Memoirs*. I felt like it was a waste of time even though the casting person did remember me from New York days! Again, I'm really not that right for the part. At night, I attended the AGA awards. Everyone was there, along with the anti-gay picketers. What a rush. Rita Moreno was superb.

Journal – Sept. 19th, 1983

It's two weeks tomorrow since we arrived in Los Angeles. We've gotten a lot done and yet I feel inactive, despondent, bitter and unfulfilled.

The apartment looks great even though it's an awful place with a terrible layout for sound privacy between the units. My days are spent in a shared environment where I lack adventure and fulfillment. I've done three interviews and one audition so far, and zilch—I sense that old waste of time staring back at me.

How long can this go on? This lack of existence, this pretense of a life, one that's not been chosen, this sense of constant compromise. To be clearer, the career and its

> *pursuit is a choice but the nature of the business is all so uncertain, based so much on chance.*
>
> *Los Angeles is a very intriguing environment. The unhealthiest I've ever lived in as far as pollution goes. The water and air quality are subhuman. They keep telling us that this is the worst weather they've ever had and I have to believe them. But does it ever really get better out here? Are we that naïve to think it gets much better? I doubt it. My three trips out here have all seemed mostly the same as far as the pollution goes.*
>
> *I have no idea about much right now. Not me, not us as a couple, not my acting and my writing, neither my future nor my past. This existence is a façade hiding erosion from within.*

Tuesday: Coo did the chorus auditions for *42nd Street*. I tried out possible outfits for *Splendora*, should auditions come down the pike later on. It would certainly be taxing doing another drag role, but for the money I'd do it, especially if the cast was decent and the project was a legitimate one. At night, I went out with Stu. Ma. to watch lousy acting scenes at Nosotros, the Latino theatre, and then we had a bite to eat. I blabbed on and on, a mile a minute.

Wednesday: Got up early to go for an EPI for Globe Theatre. I would kill to work there. Drove home and finished rereading *Maurice* to complete my St. John's College application materials. To dream or not to dream . . . Got a callback for *Listen to the Winners Shout*, not for the lead, though, but for some other role. I'm also working on pieces for Stu. Ma.'s play but it's difficult to lift that material off the page. I got a letter from Jo. H. in Santa Fe. It was short and not much to the content.

Thursday: Had my audition for Stu. Ma.'s show and they seemed wowed. I mean, embarrassingly so. They had me read for a few other parts as well. We'll believe the hype when we see a signed contract. Went shopping with Coo. Did some writing on *From Now On* at night. Picked up Da. Ml. at the airport.

Friday: Went out to Newport Beach with Coo and Da. Ml. It was a lovely day. At night, I crashed out from pills for muscle pain in my neck. Coo is going through hell these days. I can sense it, what with apartment issue and career woes. Something *has* to give. I wonder what the callback will bring tomorrow? Co. Mi. called us from NYC early in the morning.

Saturday: I went all the way out to Pasadena for a callback and again, it was such a waste of my time. I was just wrong, wrong, wrong for the part. I came back and took a look at some apartments for myself. Dropped by an ABS. Later in the afternoon we went browsing at the Beverley Center. Not bad. It's huge. Stayed in at night. We found inexpensive bottles of '78 Jordan Cabernet so we splurged and bought four more for our wine collection.

Journal – Sept. 24th, 1983

I'm trying hard not to freak out too much. Money, as usual, overshadows all of life, its wants and its needs.

I could really benefit from my own space but our finances don't permit us that luxury. God, what a lousy situation! It could be worse, but that doesn't make it better . . . nor does it change my mood.

Sunday: Another day in pursuit of finding myself an apartment. We went out to Burbank and found a few places that I liked but they're just too expensive. Dropped by Nl.'s to pay him the phone bill money from when I was out here on my own. Came back to the apartment and crashed out. I'm always sleeping these days, it seems. Spoke to the in-laws. Wrote to Se. and watched the Emmys. Another week in LaLa Land, with nothing much to account for it.

The Week of
September 26th – October 2nd

Monday: Tons of mail arrived that included unemployment insurance check for Coo and a card for me from John Scagliotti. In the afternoon we went to Ki. & Ar.'s to look over a list of agents and casting people. Must settle down to business here.

Tuesday: I spoke with Stu. Ma. early in the morning and started a mailing to industry people. At night, I went over to Mv.'s with *Journal Pornographique* and *Cooperative Murder*. He said he liked the writing a lot. We discussed the *Journal P.* and he gave me some ideas so I came home and wrote a short story as a prologue to the piece and a new haiku, "The Unknown Season," as a possible epilogue.

Toying with changing the title but not sure about it. More work obviously needs to be done.

Wednesday: Already the end of the month is at hand. I went out to Santa Monica to do a modeling booking. It was okay, even if the sets were 25 minutes long and there was only one short break in the middle of the class. I had lunch with Pt. Wh. She gave me a copy of the script. I read it and thought it was great until the end when it veered away from the original novel, an ending I didn't think played as well. It became too trite.

Thursday: Mk. Pa. called at night. It was nice to hear his voice. Can't remember what else I did today. Oh yes, I went to pick up the headshot postcards. They had placed my name on the wrong side! Went over to Academy Players and bumped into John H. from the *Rosencrantz and Guildenstern* production we'd done together back in Calgary those many years ago. Of all people. Such a small world.

Friday: There was nothing for me in the trades so I'm getting ready to do another mailing. I started to prep some of the envelopes for it; bought all the postage, enough to mail a cow. Reading *I Know Why the Caged Bird Sings*, and this gay novel, *Counter Play*.

Journal – Sept. 30th, 1983

The body seems to have a life membership to a policy of pain. My bladder is once again plagued with some kind of infection, making the rest of my system feel off. How <u>well</u> I know this scenario. Only a few weeks before my birthday and I'm riddled with complications.

> *I don't know what I want. At times it seems I just want out, deceived by the nightmare of probable options when in fact the choices are so few. The autumn starts its very real changes, even out here in this tropical climate. The weather cools and the idea of sweaters seems plausible. There's something to be said about the comfortable poverty that we have. It's not much but it's enough to survive on.*

Saturday: Another rainy overcast day so I stayed in to do my mailing. Got most of it done. Now to see what can come of this endeavor.

Sunday: Coo and I drove out to Downey to see Je. Gates' show but the museum was closed so we went off to the beach instead. Afterwards, on our return, we noticed that the tenants across the alley in the back were cleaning out their place. We went across to see their near-empty apartment and the tenants left us alone in the place to get a feel for it. We fell in love with the space but the higher rent would be a stretch for our budget.

Journal – Oct. 2nd, 2:30 AM

Just finished reading Counter Play. *What a great fantasy. How more bi-erotic can it get! And here it is in book form, light, fictional fluff, gay Harlequin romance. How realistic, though? At least it had intelligent characters to balance out the old clichés.*

Journal – Oct. 2nd, later on

In many ways, the acceptance of homosexuality is the

first sign of an intelligent heterosexual society, albeit maybe a more artistic one.

The Week of October 3rd – 9th

Monday: We went into action around 9:30 AM as Maxine was showing the apartment to prospective tenants. We interrupted our breakfast mid-bite when we saw our competition and ran like crazed fanatics, descending upon her in the courtyard as soon as they'd left her sight. We were able to resolve the situation in our favor. So . . . We are going to move. *Yet again*! We went and bought a refrigerator since the place didn't come with one. First it was another car and now a refrigerator. What's next, kids?!

Tuesday: Cathy came over at night to help us out. We did 20 or 30 hauls with her. This was at the end of a very long day of a good hundred or so trips back and forth between the two apartments. My foot feels very sore. I do hope that nothing's broken. I got two responses to my agent mailings.

Wednesday: We're still moving up and down those stairs, that's down our back stairs, crossing the alley going up a bit into the opposite courtyard and up the front steps to our new place. It takes so long. We're almost finished but not quite there yet. Saw *A Star is Born*, the new, uncut version. We went with Nl. Gosh, the man gives me angst. I modeled for a second week at Bob A.'s studio out in

Venice and dropped off the script back at Pt. Wh.'s. Will *Splendora* ever get produced, and if so, will I get to play that lead role?

Thursday: We are finally moved into our newest "new" apartment. The place is *so* beautiful. I went to meet Ri. De. at Shiloh Agency. I wasn't too thrilled by the experience. There was too much innuendo, just enough to make me feel uncomfortable. Dropped in on Stu. Ma., then went to get my foot X-rayed. Such great treatment at Mt. Sinai. The doctor was almost too concerned about my injury, as though he might have been hitting on me? Everything seems fine from what he could tell.

Friday: Went out to see Herman Zi. at his agency. He was as old, if not older than I thought, but a very sweet guy. We have a ninety-day verbal agreement. We'll see. My foot is so damn sore. I had to cancel my modeling gig, which was fine with me. Stayed in playing the invalid. Worked on my audition pieces.

Journal – Oct. 7th, 1983

It's a week before my 29th birthday. Can I be that old? It sounds old because it is old even if the face in the mirror looks rather younger. I know that that superficial feature will do its about-face when I least expect it; it will no longer be what it was, as it no longer is what it used to be.

I'm already into a second LA apartment in as many months, with a 75-year-old theatrical agent and no commercial agent, with not that much money to play

> *around with. But I persevere . . . With poetry bubbling to the surface, I look for signs that will lead me in a good direction.*

Saturday: I brought in some of our pictures that we took back in NYC to get some of them framed. It's a lot more than we anticipated. Worked some more on audition pieces.

Sunday: Went out for a mid-afternoon bite with Mv. and lent him a copy of *Z. Q.*

The Week of October 10th – 16th

Monday: Did our audition pieces at Shiloh Agency. Ri. Pa. seemed to remember a lot more about me than I would have expected. No mail, which always makes the day a bit more depressing.

Tuesday: I got a birthday card from the folks. Booked an IBM rental typewriter for next Monday. Went to library. Got a copy of *Tenth Commandment*. There's a good part in it for me.

Wednesday: We bought a nineteen-forties stove. I hope it's a good deal. I finally got a call from Bb.'s friend. I'm happy for the response but no date was set for our meeting, so we'll have to see how legit he is . . . ? Went to see *Rear Window*. I *loved* the film.

Thursday: It's the day before my birthday . . . Coo and I celebrated it at night. We went out to this Thai restaurant—loved the food. Then we came home, got stoned and opened my presents. Lovely surprises.

Friday: Got a card from the in-laws along with a gift. I went to do a modeling gig at night. It wasn't that pleasant. They wanted a slave, not a professional art model. Our new stove was delivered and installed. I got unexpected money from some of my ad sales back in Santa Fe so I went out and joined a health spa today.

Saturday: We went out to see Wor.'s play, *Men's Singles*, not bad. We were left quite alone after the performance, especially by Mat. T., so much so that Coo felt slighted by it. I wasn't sure what to make of it.

Sunday: We went out to shop and then down to Downey to see Je. Gates photo exhibit. It was interesting but not what we'd expected. Did some reading and some writing.

The Week of October 17th – 23rd

Monday: Picked up the IBM Selectric and registered for art modeling gigs at Otis Art Institute. It seems like a decent place to model. Started typing up the essays for my application to St. John's. Completed most of the material. Hopefully I can mail it out tomorrow. One small step for me, one giant step for the fate of my life . . . Monsieur called at night, much to my surprise, but always much to my liking.

Tuesday: I'm lapsing again in writing up these pages on time. It seems futile to keep a diary if I can't maintain the discipline of making accurate daily entries. I completed early morning chores before leaving to buy a sweater. Went to health spa and then finished typing up *Journal Pornographique*. Why I bothered with this one, I don't know. It's not like I'd want anyone to read this. Wrote a long letter to my in-laws. The rest of my modeling sessions out in Venice got cancelled.

Wednesday: I went to meet with Stu. Ma.'s old manager, Marie P. She was abrupt and to the point about my hair color. So . . . I came home and dyed my hair back to its natural state! Grabbed a bite with Mv. and got to meet a few of his friends. One hot, one not.

Thursday: Auditioned for LA Stage Comp. It went okay, not brilliant by any means, but okay. If nothing else, the lady was quite pleasant. She went on about my headshot. She even said she would have loved to have seen me for *Cloud Nine*. Damn, damn, damn. Cut my own hair.

Journal – Oct. 20th, 1983

The year is almost over. I am now 29 as I enter a few innocuous lines.

Having sent off my application to St. John's College, I need to start weighing out my options. I have about a 50/50 chance of being accepted according to the few alumni I've spoken with, and worse odds of successfully funding the endeavor if I do get accepted. But I'll cer-

tainly attend if I can. I've got nothing to lose in the long run, and everything to gain.

As an actor I'm not working, as a writer I'm barely writing. As a lover I don't make love. Let's go off to college!

Journal – Oct. 20th, later on . . .

I feel a need to write about how beautiful this newest apartment is. If I had to, I could live here quite happily for years to come. Though as we all know, the very definition of apartment dwelling is one of transience. The lease is just an illusion, a false hope of something more permanent than it actually is.

Friday: Long day leading to party preparations and then out to the party. Got blottoed on great grass from Mat. and Gl. T.'s pot crop. It was an interesting soirée filled with double entendres about who is and who isn't . . . gay, bi, straight! *Oy.* Drank too much. My agent Herman Zi. called in the morning for more headshots. That's always a good sign.

Saturday: Went off to the beach in Santa Monica. Stayed for a bit of sun and a quick dip. Started working on next section of *From Now On*. I've outlined most of part IV, while reviewing/editing the first three parts. I should be speaking with Mk. Pa. later on tonight. Saw one of Marie P.'s clients on *Entertainment Tonight*.

Sunday: I turn my head for one second and the day's escaped retrospection. Wednesday is already upon us as I write. I went to health spa and then off to one of UCLA's libraries. I managed to get good info from different sources to help with last part of *From Now On*. What a huge campus UCLA is. It reconfirmed for me that I probably wouldn't want to attend such a large institution as that.

The Week of October 24*th* – 30th

Monday: A full day. Went out early to copy resumes and then out to the Valley to Herman Zi.'s to drop those off. Also went by Marie P.'s but she wasn't answering the door?! Went to the health spa in the afternoon, then shopped for a decent photo shop to do our postcards. Went to an ABS. What a waste of good money. At night, had coffee with Mv. and we ended up going to this café in boys' town. He introduced me to George Maharis who was with his lover. Interesting interaction. The guy was *so* hyper, I felt quite at home.

Tuesday: Trying to settle down here to write. I did everything other than write until late in the day and then managed to write just for a bit. Pt. Wh. called. They are no longer in negotiations for *Splendora*. *C'est la vie*. I've been trying to get in touch with J. Williams in Albuquerque, but no reply. Not much mail. Got stoned at night and read up on antiques.

Journal – Oct. 25th, 1983

I haven't written much on LA, not like I did with my first impressions on New York City when I moved there in '78. It's true that as I shift from town to town, the experience of moving lessens, and with it my powers of observation, at least on an emotional level for me.

This is a lovely town that feels very unlike the major city that it is. The people, for the most part, have been friendly and cooperative. I had coffee with Mv. last night. I'm getting tired of his trying to bed me down. I'm tired of being seen as an easy conquest. That I am <u>that</u> easy doesn't help matters in the least!

But he's such a noodge about it. He's so underhanded and surreptitious in his trying to score with me; it irks me to no end. I can't help but suspect that if it weren't for this attraction to me he'd not even bother with me. That certainly is a concern. He knows a lot "about" me but he doesn't really know me well at all. We ended up having coffee with George Maharis and his lover. That was quite trippy seeing him having managed his success in the business and yet be as gay as he came off.

That's one thing that I love about LA. It's seems so much easier to meet industry people out here. Sadly, if your career is going nowhere, it means little at all in the end, except make you possibly more jealous!

Wednesday: Wrote during the day, did the gym in late afternoon and modeled at night. Coo spoke to her parents. Things seem okay for us to borrow the car to drive up to Canada if we go out there for the holidays, though they would rather we flew up there instead.

Thursday: Some monies came in for Coo. Little by little it trickles in. Got a letter from St. John's. They still need my high school transcript. Wrote to both parties to set that process in motion. Got stoned at night. I have an audition on Saturday morning for a USC student film.

Friday: A day off. Saw *Ernesto*. Loved the beauty of the landscape along with the theme. The violin sequence of seduction brought back such memories! Picked up new postcards. The layout is still just so-so. Did the gym and went to an ABS. Coo got an audition for Mark Taper Forum. Yeah!

Saturday: Went to audition for the USC student films. Not bad. Both projects had interesting premises. I came back home and spent the day writing. Worked on some Italian and Hebrew as well. At night, Coo and I went to see a movie but realized we were just *too* stoned for that endeavor so we went for a walk instead along Melrose. Stopped at this great Italian gelato place. Came home and read her some old letters from my files. We tried making love but I couldn't orgasm. How long before this is all over?

Sunday: We got up early to help Nl. move. It went rather quickly and we were back home by noon. I went to the health club. Had a quickie with this guy in the sauna room! Did some writing on my return. Worked with Coo on her audition material. Cooked a roast, watched the news and then wrote some more.

The Week of
October 31st – November 6th

Monday: We went to a pretty dull Halloween party. So much for best costume! Went through boys' town on our way home. It was a pretty crazy night in that neighborhood. Everybody was out and strutting about. We had our job interviews for the LA Renters' Lobby gig.

Tuesday: Coo had her audition for the Taper. She thought it went quite well. At night we went out on our first canvassing for the LA Renters' Lobby. It went badly. Alan and I got thrown out of Park LaBrea—not much fun for my first time out.

Wednesday: The days are spent writing and studying Hebrew or Italian. Our second night with LA Renters' Lobby was a huge success. I made very good money but I suspect it was beginner's luck first time out on my own.

Thursday: The job was a downer tonight. I finished my turf in less than two hours and I had no keys to get back into the house when I got home. I felt like I had a fever too, and was just fed up with everything. Period. Coo has a callback for the Mark Taper Forum.

Journal – Nov. 3rd, 1983

Early morning ambience—more like depression—glues me to my writing for fear of losing the last holds I have on some sanity.

These are rough times when nothing clings to anything substantive. Friends aren't writing back like they used to.

I started to do the LA Renters' Lobby last night. It reminded me of when I did the "Tray Chic" gig during my last months in NYC. It's that same aura of high energy that's needed to bring in funds in order to survive. If the Lobby does win this rent decrease we will have achieved a lot. I wonder what our pitch will be once the election takes place. I'm sure there'll be a ton of new issues to work on.

I just spoke with Co. Mi. back in NYC. Her letter of reference is going out today. It's hard to believe that she's moved out of the loft at 383 Broome Street. Everything is transient. Coo and I decided against going back east to Long Island for Thanksgiving. It's too expensive and it would be foolish of us to do that at this time.

It would be so wonderful if Coo's callback were successful. The work and the income would be a boost to our morale. I haven't received any more feedback from my second mailing to agents, not even from Bob B.'s friend, which leaves me wondering how legit the guy is, etc.

All I want now is to go off to school and be a successful student. Will this happen or not . . .

Friday: Another so-so night for Lobby canvassing. Coo and I canvassed together so it made it a little easier to take. The health spa is turning into a *mishpoocha* of *faygelehs*. Co. Mi. returned my call, and St. John's wrote to say they had received my letter of recommendation from Mrs. F.

Saturday: I'm feeling quite sick. Stayed in to sleep and nurse my cold. Got a lovely letter from Ann B. in Toronto. Read all of *The Folded Leaf*. It's certainly inspirational food to do more writing. Coo had a good audition but she didn't get the gig. It had to do with type . . . so they said. We spoke to the in-laws to tell them that we wouldn't be coming out for the holidays after all.

Sunday: Coo and I did some LA Renters' Lobby canvassing. It was easier for me to get through to people, I felt. Coo did very lousy. So what's the theory behind *this*? Umm . . . More writing done. Happy to see I can write when I want to and not having any blocks once I've committed to sitting down to the process. Ann B., Co. Mi. and Bu. Ho., they all think the Great Books Program at St. John's is a perfect match for me.

Journal – Nov. 6th, 1983

My mind races to catch glimpses of my past. So many places and times come to mind.

Ontario Youtheatre and the idea of a possible 15-year reunion brings back memories of J. Wales, the first love I had to lose. What was it that we shared in those moments of closeness, those two nights of intimacy back in '74 and again a year or so later? Was there more than lust in your heart?

I think of Gw., too, but these days, only in passing.

Then my thoughts go to my year in Montreal stage-managing at La Poudrière. What made DuPlessis act on his impulse? What was it that made what happened at the theatre on that last night possible?

Moving on to Toronto and having the great good fortune of being sent to G. Cowan's for an interview that ended up a dinner party instead. And Stan at the W. Association? What are they all up to? Would that we could go back to visit time . . .

The Week of November 7*th* – 13*th*

Monday: Another week ready to tackle at full force. Did some writing and a follow-up to my last agent mailing. Coo and I both canvassed at night. She had a good night but mine was only so-so.

Tuesday: Coo went to the dentist while I stayed home and cooked. A depressing sort of day, full of anxiety over nothing happening in our lives. I can't write more of Part IV on *From Now On* without doing even more research on social services protocols. I went to the Gay Archives to take another look at the case. I also left a message for Gloria Allred. Hopefully she'll call me back. Modeled at night for Brian, for a portraiture class. Spoke with Je. Gates.

Wednesday: Each day comes and goes, leaving its small, discernable imprint. A call, a letter, an encounter. I modeled in the morning out in Venice. Took a short walk before class to see the surf. There was a school of dolphins swimming along the coast. It was *such* a freeing sensation, watching them go up and then down below the surface, lost to the sea and its treasures. Went to health spa in the afternoon and canvassed for Renters' Lobby at night. I met a very interesting guy, a lawyer pianist at one of my addresses. We talked for quite a bit.

Thursday: Wasted the morning at Cedar Sinai clinic. It's so expensive, when all I need are my usual asthma medications refilled. On my way home, I managed an encounter with this houseboy that I cruised from my car! We went back to the house he works in and fooled around there. Talk about a very *busy* décor. The gayest décor I've seen in a long while. Canvassing at night was so-so. Mk. Pa. is finally in town. It's nice to have him around again.

Friday: The rain is still falling, steadily turning paradise into wetlands. Did some work on *The Dreamers*. Stayed in except for a visit to the gym. I got this great idea for a short story while I was there, a dirty old man theme. Need to work on it to see if it has any legs. At night, I decided not to work for the Lobby due to the weather. Went with Mk. Pa. to see two vintage Hitchcock films. Stayed up talking till very late at night.

Journal – Nov. 11th, 1983

Death is a craft where no apprentice graduates to journeyman.

Saturday: Slept in. The weather is still quite miserable. At night we stayed in to watch *Being with J.F.K*. Got stoned and was out of it, too much for my tastes. I did write a bit more of *From Now On* in the afternoon. Wrote back home after getting a letter from the folks.

> *Journal – Nov. 12th, 1983*
>
> *Watched* Being with J. F. Kennedy; *it struck me that we can never again have such an innocent time of it, never again.*

Sunday: Slept in, so very drugged out. Got ready for Je. Gates' visit. Nice company. The topics of conversation were quite interesting. One about how we, as artists, deal with the nature of our quests; and another about we, as children, and how we deal with our parents and the issue of always being a child to them, never a grown-up. Watched *Chiefs*, first of three parts. Hooked. There's nothing like deviate sex for good bait.

The Week of November 14th – 20th

Monday: If I forget, even if it's just for one day, I fall behind and the entries suffer. The week feels uncertain, even though calls from agents are slowly coming in. I made an appointment for yet another photo shoot. My life is just one session after another, here. Canvassing at night for the Renter's Lobby was okay.

Tuesday: I did a USC student film shoot. It went well though I wasn't doing much. Went to look at my budget desk commercial to see if it was worth making copies. It didn't look half as bad as I recalled. I modeled again at night for Brian. Got home in time to catch the last hour of *Chiefs*.

Wednesday: A busy day. Had an early photo session and then went to sign up for the Honda E.P.I. Came home to do some calls and then off again to an agent interview. It went so-so. We'll have to wait and see. The Honda interview was so-so as well, though I was sure they'd give me a callback, but nope, no such luck. Came home and went to the gym. Watched the last part of *Chiefs*.

Thursday: Modeled in the morning for the Venice sketch group. Did lobby work at night and picked up my contact sheets. Some of the shots look great.

Friday: I signed with the Cavalleri Agency. I hope it was a wise decision, but then again what other options did I have at this juncture?! Started typing up Part IV, what I have so far, of *From Now On*. Lobbying work was awful tonight. It was mostly all Orthodox Jews observing shabbes in the area I was assigned so I had very few takers.

Saturday: Went out for an interview for a show at the Armory. I thought it went well. Spent most of the day typing away. Got stoned at night.

Journal – Nov. 19th, 1983

These days, I long for a man like an addict his fix.

> *The need to be cuddled in the arms of masculinity pervades even my dreams and influences my daily moods.*

Sunday: Da. Ml. woke us up in the morning with a call. It was nice to hear his voice. Spoke to him very briefly. At night, we went over to Wor.'s to watch *The Day After* along with the discussion that followed.

The Week of November 21ˢᵗ – 27ᵗʰ

Monday: Another week. Went to the gym. Had a great night lobbying but it does drain you of energy. Met some nice people out there. Mv. bummed me out with his feedback on Z. Q. He said it was very muddy. It's not so much what he said, but how he said it that felt hurtful. The in-laws called us very late to tell us Fr. had natural childbirth around 12:30 AM, a little girl, Maria.

Tuesday: An eventful day. We lost the vote in city council. It was a good lesson to see how corrupt the system actually is, along with so many of the politicians. Spoke to an alumnus of St. John's. I'm going to attend another seminar in a few weeks. He sounded optimistic about my being accepted. If I do, will I be able to get the monies?! That's the even bigger question.

Wednesday: Getting ready for Thanksgiving. Lobbying at night was just a waste of time. Got onto my turf much too late. We went food and wine shopping at Trader Joe's afterwards. We had this major ordeal with a broken washing machine in the building. What a mess. We got stoned and snuck over to Wor.'s building to use their laundry room.

Thursday: A nice day. Cooked, slept and ate. Nl., Mk. Pa. and Cathy came over for Thanksgiving meal, the latter just for a short while. Things went quite well. Later on we went over to Wor.'s birthday party and had a pleasant enough time. There was this gorgeous girl from Texas there. I'm always attracted to the impossible when it comes to women, aren't I! Wor.'s brother reminded me a lot of D. Farber, and to a lesser extent, Dad, when he was younger.

Friday: Slept in recuperating from yesterday's excesses. Went to the gym. Finished typing what I have of *From Now On*. Saw *Yentl* at night. What is it about the yeshiva that so captivates me?

Journal – Nov. 25th, 1983

Just saw Yentl *tonight. It was like a jackpot for my issues. The Yeshiva with the Jewish men, the quest for knowledge, the subtleties in the attraction between the sexes, alike and opposites; it was all so intriguing.*

Hopefully St. John's will be the goyisha equivalent of the Yeshiva experience! I know I <u>have</u> to go there, more than ever before, because I have so many questions looking for answers.

Last night's dream of mental collapse, was it merely a dream or a premonition?!

Saturday: Worked on newest material for *From Now On*.

Started reading *The Bacchae* for upcoming seminar. Picked up headshots and brought them over to get reproduced. Did canvassing work for the Renters' Lobby at night.

Sunday: Wrote review/commentary on *Yentl*. Mv. critiqued it for me so now to do edits on that. Finished reading *The Bacchae*.

The Week of
November 28th – December 4th

Monday: A slow beginning to the week. I wasted a good deal of time at Cedar Sinai clinic. The cost vs. what's needed, simple prescriptions for allergy meds, is not equitable; it makes no sense. The year is winding down before our very eyes. Canvassing for the Lobby is so difficult but it's getting more automatic, pitching the request for financial support for the cause. Set about writing up the last of *From Now On*. Mk. Pa. is now apparently infatuated with Nl., of all people!

Tuesday: Slept in, so very tired. Did an early trek out to Santa Monica for my check from the Lobby. Cashed it, then went over and signed up for an audition time for tomorrow at the Odyssey Theatre. It was a very bad night of canvassing for Coo. I, on the other hand, had a good night. Dropped off my *Yentl* article to Rick. I wonder if he'll use it.

Wednesday: We went out to Santa Monica to pick up some Xmas presents from Mk. Pa.'s store, then over to our Odyssey Theatre auditions. It went fairly well but I somehow doubt anything will come of it. Luis M., from our Society of Models for Art and Education days back in NYC, was there too. Neither of us ever knew he was pursuing acting!

Thursday: I couldn't celebrate Hanukkah because we had to do canvassing work at night. I found out that Rick wants to use my article with one of my headshots to go with it. I wonder if this can move the acting career along. Can't hurt it, right?

Journal – Dec. 1ˢᵗ, 1983
Coo just received a letter from Ed K. back in NYC. He and Marcos may be splitting up. It's sad. I can tell how the news is disturbing to Coo. It just reinforces for her how precarious we are as an item.

Friday: Went to the gym in the afternoon, after wasting the whole morning waiting for headshots to be ready. They only look so-so. Joannie, at the Agency, was tactless with her lack of enthusiasm over them. I certainly got that she didn't think they would get me much career-wise! Canvassing was like death tonight. But we push on!

Saturday: Went to model in Venice. It was a nice booking. It started to rain on my way back home, which gave me a good excuse to stay in and write. At night, we saw a great show, *Penn and Teller*. Then we went with Mk. Pa. to see Stu. Ma.'s show, *In the Company of Men*. It wasn't bad. I wouldn't mind doing the show in some other context—like a larger space and some actual money! I got a letter from St. John's saying all was in and that I'd know if I was accepted within the month.

Sunday: It's the end of the year coming fast upon us. What else can I say! I went to the gym in the morning and wrote in the afternoon. D. Farber called from NYC. It was great talking to him for so long. He's in love again. Monsieur also telephoned. Such nice feelings, all from such long distances, though. The contacts made me decide to write a letter to Gw. back in Toronto. Got stoned eating our dope and did our holiday cards.

Journal – Dec. 4th, 1983

In the space of about 10 minutes I hung up from a call with D. Farber and then Monsieur telephoned. It was perfect timing to hear from both of them like that. D.'s call was quite long, Monsieur's much briefer. The latter said that he'd needed to hear my voice. After all these years, to have what we have between us is such an anchor for me.

As I speak with people and hear them talk about school, I see how very feasible that life experience could be for me. In an instant, it makes so much sense to be pursuing this for myself.

Will I get accepted, though, that's the big question.

The Week of
December 5th – 11th

Monday: (A Virginia Woolf quote started off the week in the diary: " . . . So that even if I see ugliness in the glass, I think, very well, inwardly I am more full of shape and color than ever.") What a beautiful saying. I feel that too. It was a limbo-like day with zip in the mail. No real writing and so-so canvassing for the Lobby at night. Had mild friction with Ba. All of a sudden, it appears that she's not going to cater to our needs anymore. *When* did we ask her to? I trained a new guy tonight, E. Hurd, very nice, cute, naïve and oh, so straight. So very straight. He gave me this Buddhist chant, "Nam Myoho Renge Kyo."

Tuesday: Got a call to reaudition for *Mother Courage*. Canvassing was a waste of our time, though Ba. had at least changed her attitude. What can I say, life plods onwards. Xmas gifts are off and on their way to both of our families.

Wednesday: Went out early and had a lousy night canvassing. Then I went to my callback. Talk about chaos . . . They had us all waiting outside *at that time of night* and they were running late! I heard some pretty awful actors while standing in the wings and yet they still kept making them reread the material. The AD, reading Katherine opposite us, had no idea what she was doing, and the director wasn't sure what the character of Swiss C. was going through. It made for a terrible audition experience. Welcome to Hollywood!

Thursday: Saw the short I did for USC. It was certainly a waste of *my* time. Writing is slow and sluggish. I want so much, so soon. I decided not to do Lobby canvassing at night. Got stoned instead and stayed home to relax.

> *Journal – Dec. 8th, 1983*
>
> *I elicit so many people into illicit encounters, whether in my fantasy life or in real life. If only my fantasies could suffice to satisfy my needs, I could cope and live my life so much safer compared to the chances I take, the actions that I live out.*
>
> *In the world at large, we have the animal in us . . .*
>
> *It drives a hard bargain.*

Friday: Not much during the day. I wrote a letter to Da. Ml. At night Coo and I went to the screening of parts of *Before Stonewall*. Not bad. The house was quite an interesting place, located all the way up Benedict Canyon. *La belle vie*! I think we'll send John Scagliotti some money towards it.

Saturday: It's almost Xmas time and the end of the year. Where *do* they go to?! Modeled all day at Otis. They were fairly easy classes with good teachers but the spaces to work in left much to be desired. Went to see *Fanny and Alexander*, such a masterpiece of filmmaking. The writing, the acting, the cinematography, they were all superb. Tomorrow is my *Bacchae* seminar. How will I fare? Got monies for Xmas from mom and dad.

Sunday: Went to the St. John's alumni seminar. It was a very interesting group of people with a decent discussion going on. I left my briefcase behind and will have to go back out there to pick it up tomorrow. Pam called; she and Rick want more material for the next issue of the magazine.

The Week of
December 12th – 18th

Monday: Got my briefcase back and then I drove to Pasadena to do two bookings. It's such a lovely art school up there. Did errands in the late afternoon. This was our last night at the Renters' Lobby till after the holidays. It was a lousy time with very little money collected. Though E. Hurd isn't gay it doesn't stop me from fantasizing, right!

Tuesday: A nice day. Got up early to do my audition for Mark Taper Forum. It went well. Still, my height might be an issue for the role. Bumped into Betty Garrett. It was nice to see her again. Wrote and rewrote in the afternoon, and did some typing. Made plans for Coo's Xmas tree with Mk. Pa. A few gifts arrived from Coo's side of the family.

Wednesday: Can't remember what I did today. I believe I spent it typing away like crazy and finished cleaning up Part I of *From Now On*.

Thursday: Ran errands. When I went to get the script of *Translations*, I found out they were already into callbacks. Fuck the world. Finished typing the latest draft of *Journal Pornographique*.

Journal – Dec. 15th, 1983

Pursuing an acting career is one long list of disappointments. No matter how talented you are, how talented you think you may be, there are others more talented than you.

Within a three-hour period I went from reading about Translations *being done at LA Stage Co., a theatre I'd already done a general audition for, to getting a copy of the play and reading it and feeling great about the possibility of a part in it for me, to calling them up only to find that the casting director who'd seen my audition was no longer there, but that she and the new casting person had gone through the files and already conducted auditions and were now into callbacks.*

Where do you go and what do you/can you do to get from here to there?! I've tried everything. Life with its disappointments, does it ever come out even? Can nothing be done to ensure better odds?

Friday: Returned IBM Selectric and picked up my check at Otis. Bought Xmas ornaments. At night, Mk. Pa. and I bought the Xmas tree and saw *All the Right Moves* and a *Night in Heaven*. First one wasn't bad but the second one was a real turkey. Of course, I *would* go to the bathroom when the lead shows his appendage!

Saturday: Wrote a long letter home to the folks. Decorated the tree. It looks so pretty. Coo was as pleased as I knew she'd be. We got stoned at night and went out to see Richard Pryor's new film *Here and Now*. Excellent material, as usual, very well packaged. Didn't stay up too late.

> ### Journal – Dec. 17*th*, 1983
>
> *It's been so long since love has been attached to my orgasms that I feel like a cripple, lacking in something crucial.*
>
> *By choice I refrain from making love to Coo because I don't see any future in that relationship. Wanting out because of the lack of homosexual content should be so easy to understand, so why does it cause such confusion for the both of us?*
>
> *As I see it, it's the only reality available to us. Honesty a must here, if I want to look at myself in the mirror each morning. And yet today I planned this surprise for her. I got us a Christmas tree for the first time in our marriage and decorated it for her. She'll be so surprised, and knowing her I'm sure she'll be as ecstatic as a kid. But the love she'll have for me, for my gesture, will have to be curbed from my end. It's a sad masochistic/sadistic situation for the sake of our survival.*
>
> *We do not act like animals towards each other. We are so civilized.*

Sunday: The week ends without fanfare. We decided to try and do some canvassing but it was totally dead. We came home and stayed in watching TV and reading.

The Week of
December 19*th* – 25*th*

Monday: Did my Xmas shopping for various presents and then saw *Streamers*. It was just okay. I tried to write a piece on it possibly for the magazine. Cathy came over with B. Lo. Interesting fellow.

Tuesday: We went out to Santa Monica to pick up our Lobby check and then drove all the way south to buy an electronic typewriter. Rick called to say he'd like a piece on the movie *Streamers* so I wrote one up.

Wednesday: Went to the gym. Tried to type up my article but the new typewriter doesn't work that well. Had an audition at AFI for a short tech movie. Jo. Schulman's old roommate from back in Toronto, Lynn, was helping out with the casting. That was a pleasant surprise. I thought the reading went well. Picked up a copy of the magazine with my *Yentl* piece in it. It doesn't look half bad. There's nothing in the trades again this week.

Thursday: Went to photocopy my article and rewrote the latest one. I had to return the typewriter for an exchange. The new one seems to be working very well. Touch wood! Went to various schools to look for art modeling work. At night, I went over to Pam and Rick's to deliver *Streamers* article. Got stoned and bought a Scrabble game. Found out that I got the part in the AFI film.

Friday: Getting down to the last few days before Xmas here. I went to pick up ground pork and some wine at this specialty shop. Bought some film and went to the gym. Called my sister for her *tourtière* recipe and spoke with my niece briefly. At night, I went to my first Buddhist meeting of "Nam Myoho Renge Kyo." For what it's worth, I am quite taken by the whole thing. Not so much with the singing and the whole high-energy aspect of the experience but with the simple Buddhist philosophy of cause and effect. I just hope they respect my privacy.

Saturday: Xmas eve and all that it can bring. We went out to stroll along Rodeo Drive in the afternoon and when we came home the mail had brought my letter of acceptance from St. John's! Mk. Pa. came over for a beautiful holiday meal and then we watched *It's a Wonderful Life*. Played Scrabble and decided at the last minute to go to a midnight mass that turned out to be so boring. We called up my family and I spoke to everyone gathered at the house. The three of us opened up our presents afterwards. Stayed up so late that Mk. Pa. opted to crash over.

Sunday: Woke up late. Ate breakfast and played some more Scrabble. After Mk. Pa. left we called my in-laws. Spoke to the whole clan gathered there. I also called Se. back home. He and his old friend from high school, Jy., are going to live together for a year. I think that's a good idea. Dozed on and off into the night. Merry Christmas, T.

The Week of
December 26th – January 1st

Monday: Nothing here as exciting as the London bombing raids during the war that Virginia Woolf quotes in my diary, but we have our own little foibles and traumas to work with. Filled out my financial aid forms and mailed off my letter of acceptance along with my deposit to St. John's College back in Annapolis. Once again, into the breach . . .? Went to the gym, but did no writing other than a letter to Se. So many letters written but not that many received. Life goes on, stoned and playing Scrabble. How *did* we ever live without it?!

Journal – Dec. 27th, 1983

The year is almost up and I guess this is as good a time as any to recap what's taken place. Santa Fe seems years behind us, only a minute fragment of a time span that slipped in and out of our lives.

Was it only a year ago that we were in Acapulco? Hard to believe.

Romeo & Juliet, Da. Ml., *Coo leaving for Los Angeles for that first trip, trying to rewrite* Cooperative Murder . . . *Had I begun writing* From Now On? *It will be a year this Thursday that we sold our NYC co-op. I hope we can be fortunate enough to not have to pay that enormous capital gains tax coming up.*

Santa Fe! Cold, clean, dry Santa Fe with my mo-

*torbike and those hills and my landscape job. What a
rich avenue life took us down. Coo and I, a marriage
in deep, irrevocable trouble. A bisexual man feeling the
confinements of a heterosexual marriage, caught up in a
myriad of confusing emotions. Not wanting to hurt, yet
hurting nonetheless. How does one change the life that
seems so adamant in its unwaveringness?*

*It seems hopeful, likely, that I will leave for St. John's
College back east next fall. How strange it will all be!
Is that wherein lies my life change? Will we be able to
extricate ourselves more easily from our static relationship
via this?*

*Oh, hope. That will be the guiding light for 1984.
Hope along with my new Buddhist chanting, my hard
work and the written word. I sit here feeling good. I
hope for strength and wisdom to stay with me throughout the coming year.*

Tuesday: Feeling too idle here. Sleeping in, not sure what there is to do to move things forward. Spoke to Old Globe Theatre. Their shows have no roles for me, really. I got a call from the Buddhists and it appears that tomorrow I can receive my own Gohonzon. I just hope the whole thing doesn't backfire on me somehow. Coo and I made love last night after many, many months. We also had a tense discussion about school!

Wednesday: Mid-week in the last week of 1983. Writing this on Sunday—the first day of January—adds a bit of melancholy to the entries. I received my Gohonzon tonight. It feels good and I hope to continue with this.

Thursday: Co. Mi. called us from NYC. It was great to hear from her. She had also received a copy of my acceptance to St. John's. Coo got a booking for tonight, of all times of the year! Nam Myoho Renge Kyo?

Friday: It's getting nearer. Did some shopping, sent off stuff to *Blue Boy* magazine. I started to do some more math work. Ann B. called from Toronto. I really appreciated hearing her voice and getting news from her. I'm chanting everyday. Cathy and B. Lo. came over and we tooted coke, smoked dope, drank champagne along with a good 78 Jordan cabernet. Blitzed.

Saturday: Here it is, and with it the end of a year, a book, a life so to speak with a flavor all its own. Mk. Pa. came over to play Scrabble and we toasted in the New Year with more champagne, some noisemakers and streamers. Goodbye, dear diary. I've loved your blank inviting pages and I'll visit you soon enough. Goodbye, 1983.

Sunday: (see 1984 diary)

Tobias Maxwell is the author of two novels: *The Sex and Dope Show Saga* and *Thomas*. His undergraduate alma maters include St. John's College in Annapolis, Maryland and the University of California at Riverside. He has a Master of Science in Counseling from California State University, Sacramento.

His articles have appeared in *Mom Guess What Newspaper*, *Art & Understanding* and *LA Edge* magazines.

Breinigsville, PA USA
10 April 2011
259536BV00001B/2/P